Private International Law in South Africa

Private International Law in South Africa

Elsabe Schoeman
Christa Roodt
Marlene Wethmar-Lemmer

This book was originally published as a monograph in the International Encyclopaedia of Laws/Private International Law.

General Editor: Roger Blanpain
Associate General Editor: Michele Colucci
Volume Editor: Bea Verschraegen

Wolters Kluwer
Law & Business

Published by:
Kluwer Law International
PO Box 316
2400 AH Alphen aan den Rijn
The Netherlands
Website: www.kluwerlaw.com

Sold and distributed in North, Central and South America by:
Aspen Publishers, Inc.
7201 McKinney Circle
Frederick, MD 21704
United States of America
Email: customer.service@aspenpublishers.com

Sold and distributed in all other countries by:
Turpin Distribution Services Ltd.
Stratton Business Park
Pegasus Drive, Biggleswade
Bedfordshire SG18 8TQ
United Kingdom
Email: kluwerlaw@turpin-distribution.com

Printed on acid-free paper.

ISBN 978-90-411-5180-3

This title is available on www.kluwerlawonline.com

Printed and Bound by CPI Group (UK) Ltd, Croydon, CR0 4YY.

The Authors

Elsabe Schoeman is a member of the Faculty of Law at the University of Auckland, New Zealand. She teaches and researches in Conflict of Laws (Private International Law) with a special focus on jurisdiction in cross-border litigation, as well as choice of law in contract, tort and selected areas of family law. She has a doctorate in Private International Law and has published extensively on a wide range of Conflict of Laws topics.

Christa Roodt teaches in the areas of Conflict of Laws, Conflicts Aspects of Arbitration and International Art Law at the University of Aberdeen. She has a doctorate in Cultural Heritage Law and publishes in the area of transnational commercial litigation and art disputes.

Marlene Wethmar-Lemmer is an associate professor in the Department of Jurisprudence in the College of Law at the University of South Africa. She holds a doctorate in Private International Law. She teaches in the field of conflict of laws and conducts research on conflict of laws and international commercial law.

The Authors

Table of Contents

List of Abbreviations

Am J Comp L	American Journal of Comparative Law
ASSAL	Annual Survey of South African Law
BML	Businessman's Law
BYBIL	British Yearbook of International Law
Can B Rev	Canadian Bar Review
Cape LJ	Cape Law Journal
CILSA	Comparative and International Law Journal of Southern Africa
Columbia LR	Columbia Law Review
ICLQ	International and Comparative Law Quarterly
LAWSA	Law of South Africa
LQR	Law Quarterly Review
Oxford Jour Leg Stud	Oxford Journal of Legal Studies
SALJ	South African Law Journal
SA Merc LJ	South African Mercantile Law Journal
Tasm ULR	Tasmanian University Law Review
THRHR	Tydskrif vir Hedendaagse Romeins-Hollandse Reg
TR	Tydskrif vir Regswetenskap
TSAR	Tydskrif vir Suid-Afrikaanse Reg

List of Abbreviations

General Introduction

§1. Historical Development

1. The South African legal system is known as a hybrid system. Built on a Roman-law foundation, our law has been shaped by Continental civil law, English common law and African indigenous (customary) law. The heritage of Roman-Dutch law was largely due to the establishment of a refreshment station at the Cape of Good Hope by the Dutch *Vereenigde Geoctroyeerde Oost-Indische Compagnie* (VOC) in 1652. British occupations of the Cape (the first from 1795–1803 and the final one from 1806–1910) led to large-scale infiltration and reception of English law. This continued after the Southern African colonies formed the Union of South Africa in 1910, mainly because of the ease of reference to English sources and the training of law practitioners in England. However, official legal pluralism was introduced in the colonial era when Britain retained the application of Roman-Dutch law and gave official recognition to African customary law and institutions. The establishment of universities in South Africa that taught Roman-Dutch law countered the English influence to some extent. The primary Western or European component applies alongside the local non-European customary law.[1] Furthermore, there is a universal component to South African law, which comprises human-rights law. With the overthrow of apartheid, an entrenched constitutional supreme law was implemented, aligning our system with other constitutional systems like Germany and Canada. The Constitution of the Republic of South Africa, 1996, now embodies a bill of fundamental rights, and the South African Constitutional Court has the power of administrative review. Finally, legal pluralism runs deep in the social and cultural fabric of South Africa. Ever since Muslims, Hindus and Jews entered South Africa, Hindu, Muslim and Jewish laws are unofficially adhered to by these religious communities.

2. As far as Private International Law (PIL) is concerned, South African law shares, to a large extent, the early history of Continental systems of PIL.[2] The origin of certain concepts, such as domicile, may be traced back to Justinian's *Corpus Iuris Civilis*. Many of our existing PIL rules originated during the era of the medieval statutists from the twelfth century onwards. As is the case in other areas of our

1. T.W. Bennett *Customary law in South Africa*, (2004); J.C. Bekker et al. *Introduction to Legal Pluralism in South Africa*, (2d ed., 2006).
2. For a brief history of South African PIL, see Forsyth *Private International Law*, 29–73.

law, the influence of the Roman-Dutch jurists of the seventeenth and eighteenth centuries on PIL has been immense. This was accentuated and affirmed by the frequent reference in our case law to nineteenth and early twentieth century English and Scottish case law in which references to Roman-Dutch writings on PIL abound.[3]

3. Thus it may be said that South African PIL essentially has a Roman-Dutch basis with a fair reception of English law, but in many respects English law with a strong Roman-Dutch flavour. In modern-day South African law, English law constitutes a strong persuasive comparative source of reference.

§2. General Principles

4. It is important to note that South African law is not codified. Because our common law[4] remains largely unwritten, the decisions of the courts, legislation and customary law are important sources of the law. Where statutes are available, they serve as the primary legal source, subject to the Constitution, and in that sense we have much in common with civil law systems like those of Europe. Statutes are interpreted restrictively as part of our English law heritage. However, unlike the civil law systems, our courts generally follow a system of precedent. Lower courts are bound by the decisions of higher courts.[5] For purposes of PIL, one needs to consider rules originating from the civil and common law, as well as statutory rules. Reference is often made to old sources, such as the seventeenth and eighteenth century Roman-Dutch writers. In certain areas of the law there has been statutory intervention to reform or supplement the existing common law. Ultimately, it is up to the courts to decide on the authoritative interpretation of aspects of PIL. Choice-of-law methodology relies on a comparative approach and consequently reference is more often made to comparable foreign legal systems than is the case in other areas of the law.

---

3. See e.g., *Somerville v. Somerville* (1801) 5 Ves 750, 31 ER 839; *Pottinger v. Wightman* (1817) 3 Mer 67, 36 ER 26; *Munro v. Munro* (1840) 7 Cl & Fin 842, HL, 7 ER 1288; *Forbes v. Forbes* (1854) Kay 341, 69 ER 145; *Hodgson v. Beauchesne* (1858) 12 Moo PCC 285, 14 ER 920; *Whicker v. Hume* (1858) 7 HLC 124, 11 ER 50; *Lord v. Colvin* (1859) 4 Drew 366, 62 ER 141. Reference was also frequently made to Story's *Commentaries*, which relied very heavily on civilian authority.
4. In South Africa, the term 'common law' can be used in a number of different contexts. In one context it is used to indicate the distinction between 'common-law legal systems' (i.e., Anglo-American systems) and 'civil law legal systems' (i.e., Continental systems). In another context it is used to indicate that part of South African law that is not found in legislation. More particularly, common law refers to the writings of seventeenth and eighteenth century Roman-Dutch writers (i.e., Roman-Dutch law). However, as indicated *supra*, Roman-Dutch law has also been influenced by English law. See on the use of the term 'common law': Hosten, Edwards, Bosman & Church *Introduction*, 381ff.
5. See Hosten, Edwards, Bosman & Church *Introduction*, 386ff for a detailed discussion of the precedent system.

§3. Nature and Scope

5. In the light of the mix of civil law and common law in our legal system, we are faced with two options for naming our subject.[6] On the one hand we have the Continental version of 'private international law' and on the other hand the mainly Anglo-American version of 'conflict of laws'. The term 'private international law' is acceptable insofar as it indicates that we are dealing with private-law relationships on an international level because of the presence of relevant foreign connections. However, it may be misleading since it suggests an international body of rules, common to all countries in the world, which is not the case. Each country (or more specifically, each '*rechtskring*': see *infra*) has its own national PIL within its national legal system. As far as the term 'conflict of laws' is concerned, the most serious point of criticism is that it uses conflicts or discordance between different legal systems as its point of departure and depicts each individual system as vying for its own application. This is very far removed from the ideal of choice of law (see *infra*), which is to ensure that justice is done between individuals by applying the legal system most appropriate to their case, and in a way that is aligned with decisions elsewhere in the world. The fact that an international dispute may be solved by having recourse to the most appropriate legal system among many potentially applicable legal systems, suggests that the term 'conflict' is more about choosing a legal system from among diverse legal systems than it is about conflict among laws in a traditional sense. However, the term 'conflict of laws' lends itself to greater flexibility than does 'private international law' regarding the generation of terminology for our subject, for example, conflict rule, conflicts process, conflicts justice, etc. Both 'private international law' and 'conflict of laws' are used in South Africa to indicate this area of our law, and these terms are also used interchangeably in this monograph. Where convenience and brevity favour the use of one of the derivatives of 'conflict of laws', this term will be used.

6. The Republic of South Africa consists of nine provinces. As far as substantive law is concerned, South Africa represents a single legal unit or a *rechtskring*, in the sense that it is a territory subject to a single legal system. Within the South African legal system there may occur internal conflicts between, for example, customary law and Roman-Dutch law or between religious legal systems and South African law. When courts are confronted with conflicts between two or more customary laws, Section 1(3) of the Law of Evidence Amendment Act applies.[7] The degree of recognition that courts grant to family laws practiced by migrant communities but that are not in accord with the domestic legal culture, raises questions about the scope of internal conflict of laws. Conflicts rules provide no guidance with regards to cases arising in pluralistic societies, for instance how to select among competing

6. On the naming options, see also Edwards & Kahn *LAWSA: Conflict*, para. 281; Forsyth *Private International Law*, 5–6.
7. 45 of 1988. In any suit or proceedings between Blacks who do not belong to the same tribe, the court must apply whatever law the parties may have agreed upon, be it expressly or be it tacitly imputed with reference to factors such as cultural orientation. If this cannot be done, the court must apply the law of the place where the defendant resides, carries on business or is employed. See T.W. Bennett *Customary Law in South Africa*, (2004), 69–70.

rules based on the values of a host society and rules based on the values imported by immigrant populations. As such, this aspect will not be discussed further except where internal public policy is transposed to conflict of laws. For purposes of PIL, South Africa (with its nine provinces) is regarded as a legal unit.[8] In regard to jurisdiction the position is slightly different with each division of the High Court having its particular area of jurisdiction defined. But even so, the jurisdictional criteria are largely uniform so that this does not have a major impact when jurisdiction is sought in cases concerning PIL.

7. PIL characteristically covers three main areas, namely: (1) jurisdiction of the forum to hear a conflicts case; (2) selection and application of the appropriate *lex causae* and (3) recognition and/or enforcement of foreign judgments. In South Africa jurisdiction does not normally form part of the curriculum for PIL. Jurisdiction is often taught as part of the law of civil procedure. It cannot be denied, however, that a sound knowledge of jurisdiction is indispensable for any PIL practitioner and ideally the law relating to jurisdiction should either be included in the study of PIL or be a prerequisite for the study of PIL. Certain connecting factors, such as domicile, are significant for purposes of choice of law as well as for jurisdiction.[9]

§4. Special Characteristics of National Private International Law (PIL)

8. Since South African law is not codified there is no single authoritative source of PIL. When faced with novel issues, judges resort to comparative law in action and the writings of scholars. Throughout this monograph the different areas of South African PIL will be discussed in so far as the law may be regarded as settled. Although there are many areas where authority is lacking, an attempt will be made to outline probable solutions.

8. See Forsyth *Private International Law*, 21, for a discussion of theoretically possible conflicts between the laws in different areas of South Africa. In practice, however, this will seldom, if ever, occur and therefore it will not be further pursued here.
9. Forsyth *Private International Law*, 167ff on the jurisdiction of the High Court and Harms *Civil Procedure in the Superior Courts*, (2003), paras 452ff on matrimonial proceedings.

Part I. General Principles (Choice-of-Law Technique)

Chapter 1. Sources of PIL

§1. National Law

9. This refers to our (uncodified) body of common law on the subject, as well as statute law. As far as common law is concerned, the principles of PIL are mainly derived from the Roman-Dutch writers of the seventeenth and eighteenth centuries.[10] Writers like Rodenburg,[11] P. Voet,[12] J. Voet,[13] Huber[14] and Van der Keessel[15] are important sources of conflicts principles in contemporary South African law.

10. A large number of statutory enactments relate to PIL. These include statutes designed to amend the existing common law of the country and have an influence on PIL, statutes which deal with specific aspects of PIL (including jurisdiction) and statutes that implement international conventions.[16]

11. Regarding national law in general, the most groundbreaking statutory enactment of recent times was the Constitution of the Republic of South Africa, 1996.[17] The impact of the Constitution has not, as yet, been felt directly within PIL, but it is foreseeable that the horizontal application of the Bill of Rights (Chapter 2) will affect PIL, especially in areas where, for example, gender equality is an issue.[18] Therefore the Constitution must be regarded as a source of PIL on a national level.

10. See the authorities cited in *Weatherley v. Weatherley* (1879) Kotzé 66; *Frankel's Estate and Another v. The Master and Another* 1950 (1) SA 220 (A); *Ex Parte Spinazze and Another NNO* 1985 (3) SA 650 (A).
11. For example, his *Tractatus de Iure Conjugum.*
12. For example, his *De Statutis Eorum Concursu.*
13. For example, his *Commentarius ad Pandectas.*
14. For example, his *De Conflictu Legum Diversarum in Diversis Imperiis.*
15. For example, his *Praelectionis Ius Hodierni ad Hugonis Grotii Introductionem ad Iurisprudentiam Hollandicam.*
16. References to and more detailed discussion of these statutes will be given under the appropriate headings *infra.*
17. 108 of 1996. In general, Roodt 2006 *THRHR* 546ff.
18. For instance the rule for the proprietary consequences of marriage, discussed *infra.*

§2. Case Law

12. Case law plays an important role in South African PIL. South Africa adheres to a system of judicial precedent in terms of which lower courts are bound by the decisions of higher courts.[19] Ultimately all courts are bound by the decisions of the Supreme Court of Appeal, except for matters relating to the Constitution for which the Constitutional Court is the highest authority. Therefore decisions of the higher courts and the Supreme Court of Appeal (as well as the Constitutional Court where relevant to PIL) are looked upon as probably the most important vehicle for developing our PIL. This is done in an historical and comparative manner – while due regard is had to the historical foundations of our subject, modern-day *lacunae* are invariably addressed by reference to foreign law.

§3. Customary Law

13. While there is no reason why custom should not be a source of PIL, no PIL rules originated through custom. There are many issues in South African PIL which are *res nova*; however, these will probably be solved with reference to a comparable foreign legal system or international conventions, and where authority is lacking, a decision may be based on considerations of justice and convenience.

19. See Hosten, Edwards, Bosman & Church *Introduction*, 386ff for a detailed discussion of the precedent system.

Chapter 2. Connection

§1. Conflict-of-Laws Rules

I. Total/Partial Conflict Rules

14. Conflicts rules form the basis of South African choice-of-law methodology. There are two main types of conflicts rules, namely multilateral and unilateral conflicts rules. The commonly used multilateral conflicts rule is also widely referred to as being general[20] or all-sided (in German '*allseitige*' or '*zweiseitige*'). This type of rule indicates which legal system or *lex causae* governs a particular conflicts question. The unilateral conflicts rule, on the other hand, determines when the legal system from which it comes will apply.[21] The focus of the unilateral rule is on the nature of the domestic rule concerned. As such, its content determines its sphere of operation or spatial reach.

II. Elements of a Multilateral Conflict Rule

15. The mechanics of the traditional conflict method are reflected in the structure of the typical multilateral conflicts rule. The South African conflicts rule with regard to the proprietary consequences of a marriage may serve as an example: The proprietary consequences of a marriage are governed by the *lex domicilii matrimonii*.[22]

16. The different elements of this kind of rule may be identified as follows:

- a legal category (in this example proprietary consequences);
- the connecting factor (*domicilium matrimonii*); and
- the *lex causae* as indicated by the connecting factor (*lex domicilii matrimonii*).[23]

It is possible to group the elements of this kind of rule together in different ways. First, the multilateral conflicts rule may be divided into two parts, consisting of the former, that is, the legal category and the connecting factor, as the first part; and, the *lex causae* as the second part.[24] Alternatively, one may identify the legal category and the connecting factor as the only parts of the multilateral conflicts rule, without including the *lex causae* within the structure of the rule.[25] Rabel describes the first part of a conflicts rule as a definition of its object, i.e., certain operative

20. Robertson *Characterization*, 98.
21. See Forsyth *Private International Law*, 9.
22. *Brown v. Brown* 1921 AD 478; *Frankel's Estate and Another v. The Master and Another* 1950 (1) SA 220 (A); *Sperling v. Sperling* 1975 (3) SA 707 (A).
23. This follows the structure proposed by Falconbridge *Conflict*, 39.
24. Falconbridge *Conflict*, 43–44.
25. See Forsyth *Private International Law*, 7; Edwards & Kahn, *LAWSA: Conflict*, para. 284.

facts, and maintains that the legal consequences of those operative facts are determined in the second part.[26] Rabel's approach leaves a clue as to what underlies the rather extreme view that states have no interest in the outcomes of international cases and the results of the application of a conflicts rule. South African case law does not bear this out,[27] as will be illustrated below. The consecutive stages theory provides no guidance to the court as to what weight to attach to any particular connecting factor. Criticism may be raised against categorization as a formal element of the multilateral conflicts rule or step in determining the applicable law.[28] Cases arising in an integration framework, where a decision needs to be functional in the area of domestic conflict between Member States and in relation to the intergovernmental or other institutions created for the integration, may necessitate further critical exploration of the elements of multilateral conflicts rules in future.

17. The purpose of a multilateral conflicts rule is to reveal or indicate the *lex causae*.[29] Since the connecting factor forms the link between the first and third parts of a conflicts rule, it seems that it may quite comfortably be placed with either its origin or its destination (the *lex causae* indicated by it). In line with the usual formulation of a conflicts rule, it is practically convenient to regard the legal category (proprietary consequences of the marriage) as the first part of the rule and the connecting factor (*domicilium matrimonii*) together with the *lex causae* (*lex domicilii matrimonii*) as the second part.

18. Unilateral conflicts rules are primarily of statutory origin and do not have the same structure as the multilateral rule. This will be clear from the following example taken from the Marriage Act:[30]

(1) Any person who is under the provisions of this Act authorized to solemnize any marriages in any country outside the Republic:
   - may so solemnize any such marriage only if the parties thereto are both South African citizens domiciled in the Republic; and
   - shall solemnize any such marriage in accordance with the provisions of this Act.

(2) Any marriage so solemnized shall for all purposes be deemed to have been solemnized in the province of the Republic in which the male party thereto is domiciled.[31]

19. The unilateral conflicts rule does not exhibit any distinct elements, save that it determines when the legal system of which it forms part, will apply. It is possible

26. Rabel *Conflict: Comparative*, 47.
27. *Laurens v. van Höhne* 1993 (2) SA 104 (WLD) at 121D–F; *Society of Lloyd's v. Price; Society of Lloyd's v. Lee* [2006] JOL 17577 (SCA) at para. 26.
28. Schulze 2006 *SALJ* 161 at 176.
29. Rabel *Conflict: Comparative*, 47ff.
30. 25 of 1961.
31. Section 10.

to distinguish between different types of spatially conditioned rules, namely mandatory rules of domestic law and international mandatory rules.[32] The optimal coordination between and among different legal frameworks, and between rules of different kinds and at different levels within those legal frameworks, is an important objective of conflict of laws. Regulatory challenges render it necessary to start exploring the regulatory function of South African conflict of laws in a more systematic manner.

III. Legal Consequences

20. An important characteristic of the multilateral conflicts rule is that it is supposed to treat all legal systems equally, in other words, no preference is exhibited for any one *lex causae*.[33] Because the multilateral conflicts rule regards all systems of internal substantive law to be both equal and interchangeable in principle, the *lex causae* indicated by the connecting factor may, in principle, be any legal system in the world.[34] This process ought to be neutral in the sense of being free from bias in favour of the application of the *lex fori*.[35] However, choice of law also involves matters of policy and how exactly the policy considerations of the forum are allowed to make their play. The public policy of the forum may always claim application and the forum may refuse to apply an indicated *lex causae* on the basis that such application would go against its own public policy at common law or embodied in statutory rules.[36] Moreover, in practice, South African courts maintain an interest in the outcome of the application of different *leges causae* and at times engage in a comparison of the outcomes of such application, basing their choice on policy considerations.[37]

21. The purpose of the multilateral conflicts rule is to pinpoint the most appropriate *lex causae* for a specific issue. Since this entails the ascertainment of the true seat of a legal relationship, it means that there will, generally speaking, only be one such true seat.[38] Therefore an issue pertaining to, for example, the validity of a marriage, will always be governed by the *lex loci celebrationis* in South African PIL.[39] However, there may be instances where more than one *lex causae* are available, for example in the case of the formal validity of a will where multiple *leges causae* are listed in the South African Wills Act.[40] The ratio behind this is the promotion of the

32. McClean *Recueil*, 215–217; Roodt 2005 *TSAR* 705–706.
33. Forsyth *Private International Law*, 7–9.
34. Forsyth *Private International Law*, 7; Heaton & Schoeman 2000 *THRHR* 141, 146.
35. Eiselen 2006 *SALJ* 146 at 156 as referred to by Van Heerden JA in *Society of Lloyd's v. Price*; *Society of Lloyd's v. Lee* [2006] JOL 17577 (SCA) at para. 26.
36. On public policy, see *infra* paras 70ff.
37. *Laurens v. Von Höhne* 1993 (2) SA 104 (W) at 121D–F; *Society of Lloyd's v. Price*; *Society of Lloyd's v. Lee* [2006] JOL 17577 (SCA) at para. 26.
38. See Fawcett 1991 *Current Legal Problems* 39 at 51.
39. See Edwards & Kahn *LAWSA: Conflict*, paras 306–307.
40. 7 of 1953. S. 3*bis* of this Act was modeled on the Draft Convention on the Formal Validity of Wills which emanated from the Ninth Session of the Hague Conference on Private Inter-national Law (1960) s. 3*bis* came into operation on the same day on which the Hague convention took effect, namely 4 Dec. 1970. See Corbett, Hofmeyr, Kahn *Succession*, 605–6; 621.

widest possible acceptance of formally valid wills in an international context, hence, the acceptance of connecting factors, such as nationality and habitual residence, which are foreign to South African PIL. And this in turn advances the claims of several legal systems as appropriate *leges causae*. The doctrinal assumption that every legal relationship has only one true seat is bound to come under increased pressure in the future on account of the increasing complexity of international relationships and conflicts between different levels of regulation, different structures and constellations of structures of norm-production.

22. The unilateral conflicts rule does not treat all legal systems equally. On the contrary, it dictates the application of a specific legal system when certain conditions are met. The conceptual structure of choice of law is underdeveloped in that it does not yet accommodate these rules with ready ease. Since the multilateral rule is structured in such a manner that it seeks to identify the most appropriate *lex causae* or *leges causae* in a given situation, Forsyth considers it to be more useful in choice of law. Forsyth also suggests transmutation of unilateral rules into multilateral ones.[41] However, the feasibility of this proposal is questionable. A more concerted effort to deepen and broaden the coordinating function of PIL in respect of all types of rules is likely to yield more fruit.

§2. Connecting Factor

I. Nationality

23. Nationality is not a commonly used connecting factor in South African PIL. The few instances where nationality is used as a connecting factor are based on international conventions: The formal validity of wills is regulated by section 3*bis* of the Wills Act[42] which is based on the Draft Hague Convention on the Formal Validity of Wills,[43] while the recognition of foreign divorce orders, orders for annulment of a marriage or orders for judicial separation is regulated by section 13 of the Divorce Act[44] which is based on the Hague Convention on the Recognition of Divorces and Legal Separations.[45]

24. Since the content of and requirements for nationality are unique to each country, the concept is interpreted in terms of the country whose nationality is in issue and not in terms of the *lex fori*.[46] In other words, if, for example, the question is whether the *propositus* is a national of Belgium, that will be determined in terms of the law of Belgium and not in terms of South African law.

41. Forsyth *Private International Law*, 10.
42. 7 of 1953.
43. 1960.
44. 70 of 1979.
45. 1968.
46. Forsyth *Private International Law*, 12 fn. 54. Ordinarily, connecting factors are interpreted in terms of the *lex fori*. See *Ex parte Jones: In re Jones v. Jones* 1984 4 SA 725 (W); *Chinatex Oriental Trading Co. v. Erskine* 1998 4 SA 1087(C).

II. Domicile

25. Domicile is the most important connecting factor in regard to matters pertaining to private-law status.[47] Apart from this it features as a prominent connecting factor in matters regarding movable property in terms of the maxim *mobilia sequuntur personam*[48] in general, but more particularly in matters of succession to movable property.[49] It is also the dominant connecting factor in PIL rules relating to the personal consequences of marriage[50] as well as the proprietary consequences of marriage (in the absence of an antenuptial contract).[51]

26. *Domicilium* is interpreted according to the *lex fori*.[52] Therefore, if a matter comes before a South African court, the South African law relating to domicile will be used to determine whether the *propositus* is, for example, domiciled in England.

27. Regarding the content and interpretation of the concept *domicilium*, the Domicile Act[53] is important. Until the promulgation of the Domicile Act the interpretation of the common-law concept *domicilium* was largely left to the courts. In the past, our courts relied on the definitions of domicile from the *Corpus Iuris Civilis*,[54] taking into account the expositions on this topic found amongst our Roman-Dutch authorities,[55] as well as the considerable English case law[56] on the subject. The Domicile Act eliminated a number of problems areas in regard to the law of domicile.[57] The Act does not apply retrospectively.[58] Therefore the old

47. See Schoeman *Domicile*, 12ff.
48. Forsyth *Private International Law*, 368.
49. Corbett, Hofmeyr, Kahn *Succession*, 634ff.
50. Edwards & Kahn *LAWSA: Conflict*, para. 308; Forsyth *Private International Law*, 292ff; Hahlo & Kahn *Husband and Wife*, 623ff.
51. Edwards & Kahn *LAWSA: Conflict*, para. 309; Forsyth *Private International Law*, 295; Hahlo & Kahn *Husband and Wife*, 627.
52. Kahn *Domicile*, 11; *Ex Parte Jones: In Re Jones v. Jones* 1984 (4) SA 725 (W). There is, however, a statutory exception to this general rule in regard to international competence. With regard to the recognition of a foreign divorce order or an order for the annulment of a marriage or for judicial separation by a South African court, domicile may, in terms of s. 13 of the Divorce Act 70 of 1979, be determined in terms of South African law or the law of the foreign country concerned.
53. 3 of 1992.
54. Notably C 10 40(39) 7 *pr* and C 10 40(39) 7 *lex* 1.
55. Especially Voet's *Commentarius*, 5 1 92. See also Kahn *Domicile*, 41ff.
56. Cases such as *Udny v. Udny* (1869) LR 1 Sc and Div 441 and *Winans v. Attorney-General* [1904] AC 287 have exercised a considerable influence on the interpretation of the concept *domicilium* in our case law.
57. See the South African Law Commission's Report on Domicile 1990 (Project 60) paras 1.1–1.16 (Introduction). See also the informative contribution by Thomashausen 'Reflections on "Domicile"', where the need for extensive reform of the South African law relating to domicile was explored in comparative vein, as well as Ranchod 1970 *Acta Juridica* 53; Kahn 1987 *TR* 113, where problem areas in this field of the law were highlighted.
58. Section 8(2) provides as follows:

    This Act shall not affect:

    (a) any right, capacity, obligation or liability acquired, accrued or incurred by virtue of the domicile which a person had at any time prior to the commencement of this Act;

common-law position may still be relevant in certain cases. Also, the common law will apply to aspects of domicile not specifically dealt with in the Act.[59]

28. In terms of the Act a domicile of choice is acquired when a person is lawfully present at a particular place and has the intention to settle there for an indefinite period.[60] Since indefinite period is not specifically defined in the Act, our courts will have to interpret the requisite *animus* for the acquisition of a domicile of choice in terms of our common law and decided cases. Therefore, the interpretation of the *animus* required for the acquisition of a domicile of choice has not been finally settled.[61]

29. Previously, married women and minor children (under the age of 21) used to have a 'domicile of dependence': a married woman followed the domicile of her husband[62] and a child followed the domicile of her parent (her father if legitimate and her mother if illegitimate).[63] The Domicile Act has now abolished this domicile of dependence in respect of married women, as well as minor children. The Domicile Act provides for two kinds of domicile: a domicile of choice and a domicile which is attributed to persons considered not to be competent under the Act to acquire a new domicile through choice. A domicile is attributed to (1) a child under the age of 18 years who does not have the status of major;[64] or (2) mentally incapable persons.[65]

30. According to the Report[66] the wording of the phrase, 'excluding any person who does not have the mental capacity to make a rational choice', is intended to include both mentally ill people, as well as persons who are in a protracted comatose state.[67] Regarding minor children under the age of 18 years, as well as other

(b) the legality of any act performed before that commencement. S. 8(3) further stipulates that: 'Any proceedings pending in a court of law at the commencement of this Act shall be proceeded with and finalized (*sic*) as if this Act had not been passed'.

See also paras 4.1–4.2 of the Report on Domicile 1990 (Project 60).The Domicile Act came into operation on 1 Aug. 1992.

59. For example, the interpretation of the requisite *animus* for the acquisition of a domicile of choice: see Schoeman *Domicile*, 189ff.
60. Section 1(2).
61. For a detailed investigation of the *animus* requirement, see Schoeman *Domicile*, 158ff.
62. Voet *Commentarius*, 5 1 95; Kahn *Domicile*, 73; *Weatherley v. Weatherley* 1879 Kotzé 66 at 72; *Mason v. Mason* 1885 4 EDC 330 at 336, 343; *Ex Parte Kaiser*, 1902 TH 165 at 170.
63. *Govu v. Stuart* (1903) 24 NLR 440; Kahn *Domicile*, 17.
64. The age of majority is 18 in terms of the Children's Act 38 of 2005, the relevant part of which took effect on 1 Jul. 2007. For purposes of its Project 60, the Law Commission decided that a child over the age of 18 should be able to acquire her own domicile, since that is usually the age when children leave the parental home: see paras 3.57ff of the Report on Domicile 1990 (Project 60). Although the domicile of minor children under the age of 18 years does not depend on that of their parents any longer, this category of children is dealt with separately in s. 2 of the Act. Section 1(1).
65. Edwards & Kahn *LAWSA: Conflict*, para. 297.
66. Report on Domicile 1990 (Project 60).
67. Paragraph 2.117.

persons who are not capable of acquiring a domicile of choice,[68] the appropriate section in the Domicile Act[69] reads as follows: A person not capable of acquiring a domicile of choice as contemplated in section 1 shall be domiciled at the place with which he is most closely connected.[70]

31. Previously a child's domicile at birth, the so-called 'domicile of origin',[71] depended on whether the child was legitimate (born in wedlock) or not.[72] The Domicile Act makes no distinction between legitimate and illegitimate children, since 'parent' also includes an adoptive parent, as well as parents who are not married to each other.[73] A child's domicile (of origin, or otherwise) will simply be the place with which the child is most closely connected.

32. In regard to children under the age of 18 years, the following rebuttable presumption has been included in the Act:

> If, in the normal course of events, a child has his home with his parents or with one of them, it shall be presumed, unless the contrary is shown, that the parental home concerned is the child's domicile.[74]

33. Note, in this regard, that a child does not follow the domicile of the parent with whom she has her home; the place of the parental home is her domicile. This represents a clean break with the old domicile of dependence.

34. In terms of section 3 of the Act[75] the doctrine of the revival of the domicile of origin has been abolished.[76] Whether or not this doctrine ever formed part of our law is no longer an issue; the Law Commission has done well to eliminate any

68. This refers to people who do not have the mental capabilities to acquire a domicile of choice as contemplated in s. 1: see paras 2.110–2.120 of the Report.
69. 3 of 1992.
70. Section 2(1).
71. The concept 'domicile of origin' has not been abolished by the legislator; it is, in fact, used in s. 3 of the Act. However, since the method of determining a child's domicile of origin has been changed completely, the question may be asked whether it would not be more appropriate to speak of a 'domicile at birth'. This will prevent any confusion with the 'old' domicile of origin and the way in which it was assigned to a child.
72. The domicile of origin of a legitimate child (in other words, a child born in wedlock) was that of her father at the time of her birth, while an illegitimate child (i.e., a child born out of wedlock) followed the domicile of her mother: see *Govu v. Stuart* (1903) 24 NLR 440; Kahn *Domicile*, 17.
73. Section 2(3).
74. Section 2(2).
75. 3 of 1992.
76. Section 3(2) reads as follows:
    'Notwithstanding any law or the common law, no person's domicile of origin shall revive'.

uncertainty in this regard.[77] A person's existing domicile will continue until she acquires a new domicile.[78]

35. The Act states explicitly that the acquisition or loss of a domicile is to be determined on a balance of probabilities.[79] This is in line with the standard of proof required in all civil matters. This eliminates one of the problems that has plagued our courts for so long, namely that a so-called higher standard of proof was needed to prove the loss of a domicile of origin as well as the loss of a well-settled domicile of choice.[80] In terms of the Act it is clear that, in proving the required *animus* to abandon a previous domicile, it does not matter in what manner the previous domicile was acquired (whether by choice or otherwise). Since the acquisition of a new domicile (of choice) is in many cases inevitably linked to the abandonment of a previous domicile the *animus manendi* and the *animus non revertendi* are often intertwined. Unfortunately the Act sheds little light on the contents of the *animus* requirement, save to stipulate that the required intention for the acquisition of a domicile of choice is to settle at a particular place for an indefinite period.[81]

36. In regard to choice of law, the legislator has excluded the operation of the doctrine of *renvoi* in cases where domicile constitutes the connecting factor in a conflict-of-laws situation.[82]

---

77. See the Report on Domicile 1990 (Project 60) paras 2.131–2.135. In *Ex Parte Donelly*, 1915 WLD 29 the doctrine of the revival of the domicile of origin was adopted by Mason J. on the basis of the authority of *Udny v. Udny* (1869) LR 1 Sc and Div 441, a Scottish appeal to the House of Lords. An analysis of *Udny* reveals that no Roman-Dutch authority was cited in support of the doctrine of the revival of the domicile of origin. Reliance was placed on Story *Commentaries*, paras 47 and 48 who also did not base his opinion on Roman-Dutch authority. In fact, he relied on early nineteenth-century English case law. Thus, it seems as if the doctrine of the revival of the domicile of origin was essentially an English creation. For an evaluation of English and Scottish case law on this point, see Schoeman 1994 *THRHR* 204 at 217–218.
78. Section 3(1).
79. Section 5.
80. Compare *Lewis v. Lewis* 1939 WLD 140 at 143:

    'Stronger evidence is generally required to establish a change from a domicile of origin than from a domicile of choice; but there can hardly be much difference between a domicile of origin and a domicile of choice which endured so long and became so firmly established as the defendant's Witwatersrand domicile'.
81. Setion 1(2).
82. See s. 4 of the Domicile Act 3 of 1992:

    If a court, in the application of the choice-of-law rules, finds that a question before the court should be decided in accordance with the law of a foreign state or territory on account of someone's domicile in that state or territory, the court shall decide that question in accordance with that law, even though a court of that state or territory, in the application of the choice-of-law rules, would have found the South African law or any other law to be applicable with respect to the question concerned.

III. Habitual Residence

37. Habitual residence was introduced into South African law through conventions; the first being the section of the Wills Act[83] that deals with the formal validity of Wills and which is based on the Hague Draft Convention on the Formal Validity of Wills.[84] Habitual residence is also one of the connecting factors used in the Hague Convention on the Civil Aspects of the International Child Abduction Act.[85] The Children's Act[86] has now replaced this Act. The new section 275 of the Children's Act gives effect to the Hague Convention on the Civil Aspects of the International Child Abduction, and entered into force on 1 April 2010.

38. Habitual residence is widely used on the Continent as a connecting factor for purposes of choice of law. Presumably habitual residence will also be interpreted in terms of Continental law. In this regard statements such as this part of a resolution adopted by the Ministers of the Council of Europe should be highly persuasive:

> In determining whether a residence is habitual, account is to be taken of the duration and the continuity of the residence as well as of other facts of a personal or professional nature which point to durable ties between a person and his residence.[87]

39. For purposes of South African law it is important to establish how habitual residence differs from domicile. One of the most prominent differences between habitual residence and domicile is that domicile is a legal concept, while habitual residence represents a factual situation.[88] In view of the similarity between the Continental concept of domicile ('*Wohnsitz*' in German; '*gewoonlike verblyf*' in Dutch) and habitual residence,[89] habitual residence is sometimes referred to as *domicile de*

83. 7 of 1953 s. 3*bis*.
84. Ninth Session of the Hague Conference on Private International Law (1960).
85. 72 of 1996.
86. 38 of 2005.
87. Resolution (72) 1 9, adopted on 18 Jan. 1972, quoted by Pålsson *Marriage and Divorce*, 78.
88. *Cheshire-North*, 185; De Winter 1969 III *Hague Recueil* 349 at 428; Hall 1975 *ICLQ* 1 at 9; Kegel *Internationales Privatrecht*, 345; Pålsson *Marriage and Divorce*, 77; Thomashausen 'Reflections on "Domicile"', 187.
89. See e.g., the definition in Art. 5 of the Draft Hague Convention to Determine Conflicts Between the National Law and the Law of Domicile (1951): 'Domicile ... is the place where a person habitually resides, unless it depends on that of another person or on the seat of an authority'. See also Neuhaus *Grundbegriffe*, 220 where 'Domizil' and 'Wohnsitz' are used interchangeably: 'Die Termini "Domizil" und "Wohnsitz" werden hier wie üblich synonym gebraucht, obwohl es manchmal naheliegt, das deutsche Wort für den deutschen oder die mit ihm verwandten kontinentaleuropäischen Begriffe zu verwenden, dagegen das Fremdwort den stark abweichenden englischen und amerikanischen vorzubehalten'. Compare also De Nova 1964 *Am J Comp L* 542 at 562 where he states, with reference to the increasing use of habitual residence as a connecting factor in Hague Conventions on private international law: 'Résidence habituelle, is domicile in modern garb for international consumption'.

fait and domicile as *domicile de droit*.[90] Thus, habitual residence is a concept without the legal fictions inherent in the concept of domicile: there is no habitual residence corresponding to the domicile of origin or the domicile of dependence.[91] In this sense habitual residence is a '... "virgin" concept offering greater chances to achieve international uniformity'.[92] Hall argues that, because habitual residence is a question of fact unlike domicile, it will not invite different legal interpretations from different countries and therefore a finding of habitual residence, being a factual finding, will normally not be reviewed by a forum which is called upon for example, to recognize a foreign divorce decree.[93] In this sense habitual residence will provide a connecting factor with a universal uniform meaning for purposes of private international law.

40. Having said that habitual residence is a question of fact, the issue of the relevance of *animus*, in comparison to the *animus* required for the acquisition of a domicile of choice, as we have come to know it in the common-law world, arises. There is no question that intention may play a role; however, it does not occupy the dominant position that it does in regard to domicile.[94]

41. As is the case with domicile, the requisite *animus* is often inferred from an evaluation of the relevant objective facts and surrounding circumstances. For example, it may be inferred from the *propositus*'s type of employment or from the fact that she has acquired a residence, or from other factors, such as having acquired citizenship of a country through naturalization, that she had indeed formed the intention to settle at a particular place indefinitely and has therefore acquired a domicile of choice there. This may also happen in the case of habitual residence. The actions of an individual may give rise to the inference that she has the intention to habitually reside at a particular place.[95] This does not mean, however, that an intention to reside habitually is a requirement for the acquisition of a habitual residence. As such, habitual residence differs from domicile.

42. Intention may, in certain circumstances, fortify the objective connection between an individual and a particular place for purposes of the determination of a habitual residence.[96] Pålsson gives the example of an emigrant who has just arrived in her new country and has severed all her ties with the former country.[97] On a purely objective evaluation of the emigrant's circumstances, she will not have acquired a habitual residence in the new country, while on the same facts, she may

90. De Winter 1969 III *Hague Recueil* 349 at 429.
91. In South African law the Domicile Act 3 of 1992 has abolished the doctrine of the revival of the domicile of origin (s. 3), as well as the domicile of dependence in respect of married women (s. 1(1)) and children (s. 2).
92. Pålsson *Marriage and Divorce*, 76.
93. 1975 *ICLQ* 1 at 9–10.
94. Binchy *Irish Conflicts*, 98; *Cheshire-North*, 189; De Winter, 1969 III *Hague Recueil* 349 at 430; Hall 1975 *ICLQ* 1 at 22ff; Morris *Conflict*, 23, 31; Pålsson *Marriage and Divorce*, 78ff.
95. See also Hall 1975 *ICLQ* 1 at 22ff; Pålsson *Marriage and Divorce*, 78. *44*.
96. See Pålsson *Marriage and Divorce*, 79.
97. *Ibid*., 78.

indeed have acquired a domicile of choice, provided that she has the requisite *animus* to settle in the new country indefinitely. Pålsson argues that, in such a case, the brief duration of the emigrant's residence in the new country is outweighed by the intention to (habitually) settle in the new country. However, where the objective factors alone unambiguously point to the acquisition of a habitual residence in a certain territory, there will be no need to invoke the subjective *animus*.[98] This is in line with the recommendation of the Council of Europe:

> The voluntary establishment of a residence and a person's intention to maintain it are not conditions of the existence of a residence or an habitual residence, but a person's intentions may be taken into account in determining whether he possesses a residence or the character of that residence.[99]

43. Thus it seems fair to conclude that *animus* will only play a role in the determination of habitual residence if it can be invoked as an aid to determine the exact character of the *propositus*'s residence. It also seems that, even though a habitual residence will usually be the result of a voluntary choice, lack of voluntariness may be highly relevant in regard to certain groups of individuals. Habitual residence should not be used as a connecting factor where residence is involuntary. It is therefore submitted that, while voluntariness should not constitute an essential requirement for the acquisition of a habitual residence, forced residence, in the sense that the individual has no freedom of choice in regard to where she wishes to settle, will definitely negate the acquisition of a habitual residence. However, with habitual residence the emphasis is on the factual situation and therefore the objective facts and surrounding circumstances will, in the absence of strong evidence to the contrary, be decisive.

IV. Residence *Simpliciter*

44. This is the most basic or simple form of residence and amounts to nothing more than physical presence at a particular place which is not merely fleeting or transitory.[100] It is not necessary to reside in a house or even to have a roof over one's head. There must, however, be some degree of permanence. This may be proven by the fact that the *propositus* has a real interest in residing at a certain place,[101] for example a building contractor who builds a house for someone and resides at that place for the duration of the building operations. Even though an *animus*, such as that required for the acquisition of a domicile of choice, is not a requirement for residence *simpliciter*, the intention of the *propositus*, which may be deduced from certain factors, such as the signing of a lease for a certain period, may serve to

98. See also De Winter 1969 III *Hague Recueil* 349 at 430 who says that a person's hidden mental attitude cannot affect the determination of his habitual residence in the face of conclusive objective facts.
99. Resolution (72) 1 10, adopted on 18 Jan. 1972, quoted by Pålsson *Marriage and Divorce*, 79.
100. McClean 1962 *ICLQ* 1153 at 1154.
101. Forsyth *Private International Law*, 206.

qualify the degree of permanence of his residence.[102] It also matters not whether the *propositus* resides at a particular place of his own volition. The rationale behind this is that insistence on voluntary residence would prevent individuals such as prisoners from having a residence *simpliciter* and thus, where residence *simpliciter* constitutes a ground of jurisdiction they will be precluded from the court's jurisdiction. This will have the effect of placing them in a privileged position, free from the jurisdiction of the court.[103] Actual physical presence forms the essence of residence *simpliciter*: If this link is severed, there is no additional requirement, such as intention, to constitute residence *simpliciter*. Where ordinary residence is a basis for the jurisdiction of a court, multiple residences are ruled out.[104] In England and Canada, where the courts have adopted the real home as the test of ordinary residence, the inference is strong that the inquiry must be directed at finding the one true home among several places of residence.[105]

45. Since residence *simpliciter* is mainly used in statutes, it should be interpreted in terms of the intention of the legislator.[106] In South African law residence has up until now been used as a jurisdictional connecting factor. The Supreme Court Act[107] provides that: 'A provincial or local division of the Supreme Court shall have jurisdiction over all persons residing or being in ... its area of jurisdiction ...'[108] This section means that a court may have jurisdiction in relation to a matter even though the cause had not arisen within its area of jurisdiction, provided it has jurisdiction over the person of the defendant. However, it does not mean that the court of a defendant's residence is competent to hear a case as a matter of principle.[109]

46. The term 'residing' is not defined in the Act. The determination of a person's residence is a factual enquiry. The courts have been reluctant to formulate an all-embracing definition of the concept.[110] What has emerged is that a person may have a domicile in one place and reside for the time being in another; may have more than one residence and does not reside at a place she is temporarily visiting, nor does she cease to reside at a place merely because she is temporarily absent on certain occasions and for short periods.[111] Residence *simpliciter* is primarily used as a statutory jurisdictional criterion.

102. McClean 1962 *ICLQ* 1153 at 1156.
103. *Ibid.*, 1159. Historically, the jurisdiction of ecclesiastical courts was based on residence: *Niboyet v. Niboyet* (1878) 4 PD 1 at 5.
104. Castel *Canadian Conflict*, 4.22.
105. See Castel *Canadian Conflict*, 4.22.
106. *Ibid.*, 94; Forsyth *Private International Law*, 206.
107. 59 of 1959 (which regulates conduct in the High Court).
108. Section 19(1)(a). See also s. 29 (1) of the Children's Act 38 of 2005 which refers to the children's court of the district in which the child is ordinarily resident for the purposes of assumption of jurisdiction.(Child Care Act repealed by Children's Act from 1 Apr. 2010).
109. Harms *Civil Procedure* A4.12, 16.
110. Harms *Civil Procedure* A4.12, 16; *Mayne v. Main* [2001] 3 All SA 157 (A); 2001 2 SA 1239 (SCA); Morris *Conflict*, 20.
111. *Bisonboard Ltd. v. K. Braun Woodworking Machinery (Pty) Ltd.*, 1991 (1) SA 482 (AD) at 492H–I also Binchy *Irish Conflicts*, 101.

47. Ordinary residence seems to connote physical residence in a particular place for settled purposes. This does not mean that there must be continuous physical presence; accidental or occasional temporary absences will not have any effect on ordinary residence. Generally speaking, ordinary residence refers to the regular order of an individual's life for the time being and it does not matter that the residence may be of short duration.[112] In comparison to domicile, no intention to settle indefinitely, in the sense of the *animus* required for the acquisition of a domicile of choice, is required. As was the case with residence *simpliciter*, the intention of the *propositus*, as manifested by her acts, such as enrolment at a university and residing at a university residence, may qualify her residence as having been adopted for settled purposes.[113]

48. The distinction between residence *simpliciter* and ordinary residence probably lies in the degree of permanence or continuity. Residence *simpliciter* refers to residence for the time being (and may, in this sense, pertain to a specific purpose), while ordinary residence pertains to the way in which an individual orders her life. Therefore, ordinary residence will not be relinquished by temporary absences, while such absences may actually terminate residence *simpliciter*. In this sense ordinary residence refers to the place in which the individual lives and works and the society within which she moves on a daily basis. There seems to be confusion in regard to the question whether voluntariness should be a prerequisite for ordinary residence. As is the case with residence *simpliciter*, McClean argues that voluntariness is not essential for ordinary residence,[114] while the authors of Morris *Conflict*[115] incorporate 'voluntary' into their definition of ordinary residence. Nygh, on the other hand, qualifies 'voluntary' to the extent that the residence must not be the result of kidnapping or imprisonment.[116]

49. Ordinary residence is used as a jurisdictional connecting factor by the South African legislator in the Divorce Act.[117] A court will have divorce jurisdiction if the parties or either of the parties is: ... ordinarily resident in the area of jurisdiction of the court on the said date and have or has been ordinarily resident in the Republic for a period of not less than one year immediately prior to that date.[118]

50. No definition of ordinary residence is given in the Act; therefore the concept must be interpreted with due regard being had to the intention of the legislator, as well as existing definitions and interpretations of the concept. Since the aim of this

112. Binchy *Irish Conflicts*, 101; *Cheshire-North*, 184; Fawcett 1962 *ICLQ*, 1153 at 1161; Morris *Conflict*, 20.
113. Nygh *Conflict*, 267.
114. 1962 *ICLQ* 1153 at 1162. See also Binchy *Irish Conflicts*, 102–103 who, with reference to Irish case law, comes to the same conclusion, as well as De Jager (*Domicilium as Koppelfaktor*, 218 fn. 2) who argues that the absence of volition constitutes the main difference between ordinary residence and habitual residence.
115. 20.
116. *Conflict*, 266. See also *Cheshire-North*, 183.
117. 70 of 1979.
118. Section 2(1)(b). Section 2(1)(a) deals with jurisdiction founded on the domicile of the parties.

section is to enable a court to assume jurisdiction in divorce cases more readily,[119] ordinary residence will be interpreted rather leniently.

V. *Lex Loci Actus*

51. *Lex loci actus* refers to the law of the place where a transaction took place and, as such, the *locus actus* is used as a connecting factor in the areas of family law, law of succession and the law of contract. However, determining where exactly the *locus contractus* is in regard to contracts may often be difficult, since modern means of communication make it possible to conclude contracts over the Internet or by offer and acceptance through the mail. In South African law a contract is concluded where and when the offer is posted,[120] but this may differ from other legal systems and may make international harmony of decision hard to achieve. Also, in modern times the place where a contract is entered into may be completely fortuitous, so that it does not establish a significant connection with the contract at all.[121]

VI. *Lex Rei Sitae*

52. The *lex rei sitae* is generally used to indicate the legal system that governs conflicts issues related to immovable property, that is the law of the place where such immovable property is situated. The underlying rationale for this rule is that jurisdiction over immovable property usually vests in the court of the place where such property is situated and that this is the only court that can give an effective judgment regarding such property.[122]

VII. Intention of the Parties

53. The intention of the parties plays an important role in regard to contracts in terms of the principle of party autonomy.[123] Where there is an express or implied choice of law in a contract, this will be followed unless there exist compelling considerations of, for example, public policy, which militate against the application of the chosen law.[124] Where there is no express or tacit choice of law by the parties, the proper law of the contract must be determined. Even though current trends point to an objective determination of the proper law of a contract,[125] the leading South

119. One of the policies underlying divorce jurisdiction is to assume jurisdiction whenever possible: Fawcett 1985 *Oxford Jour Leg Stud* 378 at 381.
120. See Forsyth *Private International Law*, 333.
121. *Ibid.*
122. Forsyth *Private International Law*, 369. Harms *Civil Procedure* A4.12 at 16.
123. Forsyth *Private International Law*, 325–326.
124. Edwards & Kahn *LAWSA: Conflict*, para. 329. See further *infra* paras 70ff; Forsyth *Private International Law*, 327.
125. *Ibid.*, para. 330. See further *infra* paras 104ff.

African case on the subjective-intention theory for contracts has not been authoritatively rejected. In terms of this approach it must be determined 'what ought ... to be presumed to have been the intention of the parties'.[126]

§3. Changes in the *Lex Causae*

54. There has only been one case before our courts in which there was a change in the *lex causae*, namely *Sperling v. Sperling*.[127] In this case a couple married in the former East Germany, their matrimonial domicile being East Germany as well. They subsequently settled in South Africa where they acquired a domicile of choice. Upon divorce in a South African court, the issue of a change in the *lex causae* (an intertemporal conflict) arose. As the *lex domicilii matrimonii* the law of East Germany governed the proprietary consequences of their marriage.[128] However, after they had already moved to South Africa, the law of East Germany changed by introducing a partial community-of-property regime into the *ex lege* out-of-community regime and this legislation was given retrospective effect. The question was whether the old or the new law of East Germany should be applied. Corbett J.A. decided that the changed *lex causae* should apply on the basis of the balance of justice and convenience. Also, the application of the changed *lex causae* was not against public policy in this instance.[129] The decision in this case does not mean that the changed *lex causae* will always be applied in such cases; it will depend on the balance of justice and convenience, as well as considerations of public policy.

§4. Combination of Connecting Factors

55. Generally speaking, combinations of connecting factors are rare in South African PIL. An example of cumulative bilateral reference is found in South African succession law. Several connecting factors are employed to determine the formal validity of a last will and testament in respect of movables (seven connecting factors)[130] and immovables (eight connecting factors).[131] Domicile and citizenship are combined in a statutory unilateral conflicts rule relating to the formal validity of marriage:

(1) Any person who is under the provisions of this Act authorized to solemnize any marriages in any country outside the Republic:
   (a) may so solemnize any such marriage only if the parties thereto are both South African citizens domiciled in the Republic; and

126. *Standard Bank of South Africa Ltd. v. Efroiken and Newman* 1924 AD 171 at 185.
127. 1975 (3) SA 707 (A).
128. *Frankel's Estate and Another v. The Master and Another* 1950 (1) SA 220 (A).
129. At 724D.
130. Section 3*bis* (1)(a) of the Wills Act 7 of 1953.
131. Section 3*bis* (1)(a) and (b) of the Wills Act 7 of 1953; *Tomlinson v. Zwirchmayer* 1998 (2) SA 840 (T).

(b) shall solemnize any such marriage in accordance with the provisions of this Act.

(2) Any marriage so solemnized shall for all purposes be deemed to have been solemnized in the province of the Republic in which the male party thereto is domiciled.[132]

In cases involving sales transactions in which a particular state has a vital cultural interest, cumulative reference rules are potentially useful.[133]

132. Section 10 of the Marriage Act 25 of 1961.
133. Roodt 2003 *CILSA* 9.

Chapter 3. Basic Terms

§1. Characterization (Classification)

56. Internationally, the literature on characterization is extensive. All the major works on the conflict of laws contain a section on characterization [also termed qualification after its French origins (*qualifikation* in German), or classification].[134] Classification lies at the basis of every choice-of-law decision adopted by a South African court. The problem of characterization is best understood with reference to the multilateral conflicts rule that takes the form of a legal category and a connecting factor indicating the applicable *lex causae*.[135] Whereas it may be easy to determine the legal category in the majority of cases, for example, validity of marriage or capacity to inherit under a will, it may be more difficult to decide whether an issue falls within the legal category of proprietary consequences of marriage or within the legal category of *succession* where a marriage is terminated by the death of one of the spouses.[136] A dispute could well be subsumable under more than one choice-of-law category in classification.[137] Characterization easily creates hardship for litigants.[138] While the problem of characterization was present in the earlier South African cases, it was not identified and discussed as such.[139]

57. Scholarly commentaries on conflict of laws cover the whole range of theories and approaches to characterization.[140] A number of scholars adopt the view that

134. See e.g., *Cheshire-North*, 41ff; *Dicey-Morris Vol. 1*, 37; Morris *Conflict*, 503ff; Falconbridge *Conflict*, 50ff; Kahn-Freund *General Problems*, 223ff; Neuhaus *Grundbegriffe*, 113ff. See also the following contributions: Beckett 1934 *BYBIL* 46; Lederman 1951 *Can B Rev* 3; 168; Morse 1949 *Columbia LR* 1027 (especially fn. 3 which contains an extensive list of references to writings on the question of characterization).
135. See *supra* paras 15ff.
136. See e.g., *Anderson v. The Master* 1949 (4) SA 660 (E) (which involved the question whether *ius relictae* (in terms of Scots law) should be classified as proprietary consequences of marriage or as succession).
137. Corbett 1993 *TSAR* 1 at 5. Roodt 2006 *THRHR* 215; 367 and 546 respectively.
138. See fn. *supra*, as well as the following examples: *Gaarn v. Cairn's Executors* 1910 EDL 462 (where a child's claim to a *legitim* under Scots law was classified as a proprietary consequence of the parents' marriage); *Powell v. Powell* 1953 (4) SA 380 (W) (where the erstwhile South African prohibition on donations between spouses was classified as a personal, rather than a proprietary, consequence of marriage); *Pitluk v. Gavendo* 1955 (2) SA 573 (T) (where the then Rhodesian rule that marriage revokes previous wills was classified as a proprietary consequence of marriage); *Perrot-Humphrey v. Perrot-Humphrey* 1967 (3) SA 304 (W) (where the then South African right of recourse against the other spouse for household necessaries was classified as a personal, and not a proprietary, consequence of marriage).
139. Forsyth *Private International Law*, 88-89.
140. Edwards & Kahn *LAWSA: Conflict*, para. 285; Eiselen 2006 *SALJ* 146; Forsyth 1987 *SALJ* 4; Forsyth 2006 *Journal of Private International Law* 169, 172n16; Forsyth *Private International Law* at 76ff; Schulze 2006 *SALJ* 161, Neels 2003 *SALJ* 883; Hahlo & Kahn *Husband and Wife*, 578ff; Corbett, Hofmeyr, Kahn *Succession*, 591ff; Neels 2008 *Journal of Private International Law* 167; Bennet & Kopke 2008 *SALJ* 62.

it is rules of law that are classified and not concrete factual problems at hand.[141] No decision of the Supreme Court of Appeal expressly confirms this view, however, and not everyone agrees with it.[142] Classification used to be done *lege fori*, that is: the categories of the *lex fori* (South African law) determined how foreign rules (or: legal issues, depending on the approach one takes with respect to the object of classification) were to be classified.[143] Recently the courts indicated that the classification adopted by the foreign legal system may also be relevant.[144]

58. Forsyth's view that it is rules of law which must be classified was confirmed by Booysen J. in the Supreme Court, Durban and Coast Local Division in *Laconian Maritime Enterprises Ltd. v. Agromar Lineas Ltd.*[145] The South African court was approached for an order that an arbitration award handed down in London be made an order of court in terms of the recognition and enforcement of Foreign Arbitral Awards Act 40 of 1977. One of the defences raised against the enforcement of the award was that of prescription. The proper law of the arbitral award was English law and in terms of the English law at that time, their rules of prescription were regarded as being procedural in nature. The South African rules of prescription, on the other hand, were substantive in nature.[146] Since neither the English rules were applicable (a South African court cannot apply foreign procedural rules), nor were the South African rules (on the basis of the argument that South African law was not the *lex causae*), the court concluded that the phenomenon of 'gap' had arisen. On the basis of his oath as a judge enjoining him to apply his own country's law, Booysen J. decided to apply the South African prescription rules (the *lex fori*) in an ad hoc decision.[147] The claim had not prescribed according to either English or South African law. Consequently, the choice of law would not have made a real difference to the outcome in this instance. This could be the real reason for the judge's readiness to resort to the *lex fori*, for he specifically declared that classification is done in terms of the *lex fori*.[148] However, as pointed out by Forsyth, Booysen J. did not follow the strict *lex fori* approach, but, taking into account the nature of the English rules of prescription and their characterization in English law, may be said to have applied an enlightened *lex fori* approach or even a *via media* approach to

141. Forsyth 1987 *SALJ* 4; Forsyth 2006 *Journal of Private International Law* 169, 172n16; Forsyth *Private International Law* at 78; Also Edwards & Kahn *LAWSA: Conflict*, para. 285; Neels 1993–2000 at 2; Schulze 2006 *SALJ* 173.

142. For instance Eiselen 2006 *SALJ* 146 at 148 holds that the cause of action is the actual object of classification. Bennet & Kopke 2008 *SALJ* 62 also seem to be of this opinion.

143. Except for *Anderson v. The Master* 1949 4 SA 660 (E) where classification took place in terms of the *lex causae*.

144. *Kuhne v. Nagel AG Zürich v. APA Distributors (Pty) Ltd.* 1981 (3) SA 536 (WLD) 539D–E; *Laconian Maritime Enterprises Ltd. v. Agromar Lineas Ltd.* 1986 (3) SA 509 (D & CLD) at 518Hff; *Laurens v. Von Höhne* 1993 (2) SA 104 (W); *Parry v. Astral Operations Ltd.* [2005] 10 BLLR (LC) at §41.

145. 1986 (3) SA 509 (D) at 518B; 519I.

146. See *Kuhne and Nagel AG Zürich v. APA Distributors (Pty) Ltd.*, 1981 (3) SA 536 (W).

147. At 524F.

148. At 521A.

classification.[149] The 'residual *lex fori*' approach was followed in two other instances.[150]

59. In *Laurens v. Von Höhne*[151] Schutz J. expressly adopted the *via media* technique of classification, as formulated by Falconbridge in the 1950s[152] and propagated by South African scholars.[153] This case concerned the questions whether (1) the defendant had in fact paid his contribution towards the outstanding share capital of a German company, and, if not, (2) whether a claim for such payment had become prescribed. Schutz J. maintained with reference to Turpin that the conflict rules of the forum should be construed from a cosmopolitan or worldwide point of view, so as to be susceptible to application of foreign domestic rules.[154] He adopted a *via media* approach and decided that the rules regarding payment of share capital should be considered within the context of that particular legal system, paying full attention to the nature, scope and purpose of these rules in their foreign-law context. Schutz J. stressed that he was not concerned with what had to be proved (clearly, that was whether payment had been made), but how it should be proved and this was a procedural matter governed by the *lex fori*. He decided as a matter of policy that South African law must determine whether payment had been made.[155] The issue of prescription did not raise any difficulties in this case. Applying the *via media* approach it was decided that German law characterized their rules of prescription as substantive even though they were only remedy-barring. While these rules could be regarded as weak and be classified as procedural in terms of South African law, the judge stated that the South African Act is classified as substantive 'so that it is not a matter for the *lex fori*'.[156] Since German law, as the *lex causae*, governed substantive matters, the German rules of prescription were applied. As in *Laconian*, there was no conflict between the potentially applicable systems of law in this instance. Judge Schutz also noted that this case differed from the *Laconian* case in that it posed no temptation to apply the residual *lex fori* approach.[157]

60. In *Society of Lloyd's v. Price*; *Society of Lloyd's v. Lee*[158] Lloyd's had instituted separate claims for provisional sentence against two Lloyd's names, Price and Lee. Default judgments had been obtained against them in 1997 in the Queen's

149. See Forsyth 1987 *SALJ* 4 esp. 10–11.
150. Minister of Transport, *Transkei v. Abdul* 1995 (1) SA 366 (N); *Society of Lloyd's v. Price and Lee* 2005 (3) SA 549 (T). Forsyth 2006 *Journal of Private International Law* 169 criticizes the latter case.
151. 1993 (2) SA 104 (W).
152. Falconbridge *Conflict* 59.
153. J. Booysen, refers to, among others, Kahn *Appendix: Succession* 620–621; Turpin 1959 *Acta Juridica* 222. In general also Neels 1993–2000 at 2; Neels 2008 *Journal of Private International Law* 167.
154. At 116I–J.
155. At 121A–B.
156. At 121D–E.
157. At 121E–F.
158. *Society of Lloyd's v. Price; Society of Lloyd's v. Lee* [2006] JOL 17577 (SCA) at para. [12]. In general, Forsyth 2006 *Journal of Private International Law* 425; Neels 2007 *TSAR* 178.

Bench Division of the High Court of Justice in London for non-payment of the so-called *equitas premium*, payable by all members who did not accept the settlement of claims under Lloyds' 1993 Reconstruction and Renewal Plan. Both names were resident in South Africa and Lloyd's sought to enforce the judgments in South Africa. Each defendant had entered into a General Undertaking with Lloyd's that contains both a choice-of-law clause (i.e., that the Undertaking shall be governed by and construed in accordance with the laws of England) and a choice of venue clause (i.e., that the courts of England shall have exclusive jurisdiction to settle any dispute arising from or relating to Lloyd's membership or the underwriting of insurance business). The real issue was whether the judgments were prescribed. In this case, a conflict between the potentially applicable systems of law in regard to the classification of prescription rules presented itself. The default judgments were obtained in an English court less than six years before the provisional sentence summonses were served on the defendants in South Africa. In terms of section 24 of the English Limitation Act of 1980, the claims on the judgments would not have become statutorily prescribed. However, since more than three years had passed since the default judgments were obtained, the outcome would be different if the three-year prescription period of section 11(d) of the South African Prescription Act 68 of 1969 were to be applied. The court *a quo* dismissed the claims on the grounds that they had become prescribed in terms of the South African Prescription Act 68 of 1969. The Supreme Court of Appeal referred to the potential conflict between the legal systems and resorted to the steps associated with *via media* classification of *Laurens NO v. Von Höhne*.[159] The Court of Appeal concluded that, at the basis of the case, prescription is a matter of substance under the *lex fori*, but a matter of procedure under the *lex causae*, and assumed that this gives rise to gap.[160] It held that English law was applicable.[161] English law not only governed the creation, operation, interpretation and enforcement of the rights of the parties,[162] but also had the closest and most real connection with the question of the extinction or non-enforceability of such rights. Moreover, the court referred to the artificiality of the traditional distinction between extinctive and remedy-barring statutes of limitation.[163] The judgment claims were held to be alive and enforceable.

61. In *Society of Lloyd's v. Romahn*,[164] Lloyd's sought, once more, to enforce judgments obtained in London against names resident in the Cape Province in South Africa. The points arising were identical to those in *Price and Lee*. Van Zyl J. handed down his decision after the first instance had decided that case, but before the SCA had the opportunity to do so, proposing a residual *lex causae* approach to

---

159. At paras 14–17.
160. At paras 21–22. The assumption is that the South African law governed only procedure and the English law only governed substance. In general also Neels 2003 *SALJ* 889–891; Forsyth 2006 *Journal of Private International Law* 426.
161. At para. 31.
162. At para. 28.
163. *Ibid.*
164. Reported *sub nom. The Society of Lloyd's v. Ilse* 2006 CLR 101 (C). In general Forsyth 2006 *Journal of Private International Law* 427.

resolving gap. He based this decision on fairness, reasonableness and policy considerations.[165]

62. In view of the important role that court decisions play in the development of South African PIL, the *via media* approach to classification is the approach that will be followed in future. Forsyth insists on asking whether the relevant rules of English and South African law concerning prescription (or limitation) relate to substance or procedure.[166] Eiselen ascribes the dilemma in *Laconian* to the double classification of certain rules on the basis of the false premise that the object of classification was the legal rule and adhering to rule selection.[167] In his view, the true object of classification is the cause of action or the issue concerned, and since the jurisdiction-selection approach underlies choice of law in South Africa, the courts are not concerned with rules, nor should they be.[168] Classification is called for as a single, rather than a double, step, as was done in *Laurens v. Von Höhne.*[169] The *via media* approach complicated the court's argument unduly. Comparative law and experience indicates that, in order to ensure that rights still in existence in a foreign country are not nullified, and claims that are non-existent at the source are not enforced in the domestic forum, prescription is best classified as substantive.[170]

§2. Preliminary Question

63. The preliminary question (or incidental question) arises in a conflicts problem, apart from the main question which must be decided. Let us take an example. M, who lived alone, dies intestate while domiciled in country A. His estate consists of movable property only. W claims she and M were married in country B ten years before his death and that she is entitled to a certain portion of his estate. M's family disputes the validity of the alleged marriage. In this case the main question is intestate succession to movable property and the preliminary question concerns the validity of W's alleged marriage to M. This preliminary question must be resolved before the main question can be decided. In terms of South African PIL intestate succession to movables is governed by the *lex ultimi domicilii*, which in this instance will be the law of country A. Further, it appears that, in terms of South African PIL the validity of the alleged marriage is governed by the *lex loci celebrationis*, in this instance the law of country B, while, in terms of the PIL of the *lex causae* of the main question (the law of country A) the validity of the marriage is governed by the *lex patriae*, let us say in this instance the law of country C. There is no authoritative court decision on the preliminary question in South African PIL, given that the problem is seldom recognized, but, with reference to the hypothetical

165. Paragraph 86.
166. Forsyth 2006 *Journal of Private International Law* 426.
167. At 147, 153, 155, 158.
168. At 155. But see *Laurens v. Von Höhne* 1993 (2) SA 104 (W) at 121A; *Society of Lloyd's v. Romahn* 2006 (4) SA 23 (CPD) at para. 86; *Sadiku v. Sadiku* unreported, Case No. 30498/06 (TPD).
169. At 154, 157, 159.
170. Roodt 2007 *Yearbook* 372.

scenario *supra*, commentators on the conflict of laws agree that the following requirements must be met for a true preliminary or incidental question to arise.[171] First, there must be a principal (main) question which is, in terms of the relevant conflicts rule of the forum, governed by a foreign legal system. For example, the succession to movable property in our example above is governed, in terms of South African PIL, by the *lex ultimi domicilii*, the law of country A. Second, there must be a subsidiary or an incidental or a preliminary question in the same case which could constitute a principal question on its own and has its own conflicts rule. In our example it is the validity of the marriage and this is governed, in terms of South African PIL, by the *lex loci celebrationis*, the law of country B. Third, the application to the incidental question of the conflicts rule of the foreign *lex causae* of the main question, must produce a result different from the application to the incidental question of the *lex causae* indicated by the conflicts rule of the forum. In other words, there is a conflict between the conflicts rules of the forum and the *lex causae* of the main question as far as the resolution of the incidental question is concerned. In our example this would mean that, in terms of the forum's conflicts rule, the validity of the marriage is governed by the *lex loci celebrationis*, the law of country B, while, in terms of the PIL law of country A (the *lex causae* of the main question) the validity of the marriage is governed by the *lex patriae*, the law of country C, with different results.

64. Once a true incidental question has been identified, the problem is to decide whether the incidental question should be determined by the conflicts rules of the law governing the main question ('dependent application' or 'wide reference' approach) or by the conflicts rules of the forum ('independent determination' or 'narrow reference' approach). On this issue opinion remains divided.[172]

The decision in *Phelan v. Phelan*[173] warrants mentioning in this regard. In this case, the plaintiff (Ms Phelan) instituted action in the Cape High Court against Mr Phelan for divorce, custody of their three children and maintenance for herself and the children. The defendant averred that no valid marriage was concluded between himself and the plaintiff. The plaintiff and defendant were both previously married to other partners and both obtained divorce orders from their previous spouses in the Dominican Republic whilst citizens of and domiciled in the Republic of Ireland. At that time divorce was not recognized in Ireland. Thereafter the plaintiff and defendant underwent a marriage ceremony in Australia whilst still domiciled in Ireland. The inherent validity of the marriage concluded in Australia has to be determined in accordance with the *lex loci celebrationis*, i.e., the law of New South Wales, Australia. The validity of the Australian marriage was dependent upon the

171. Edwards & Kahn *Conflict: LAWSA*, para. 287; Forsyth *Private International Law*, 103ff; Neels 1993 *TSAR*, 760. See also *Cheshire-North*, 51ff; Morris 496ff; Schuz *Incidental Question*, 3–4.

172. Forsyth *Private International Law* 105 opts for a 'nonmechanical' approach. Shuz *Incidental Question* 5 and 68ff proposes a result-selecting approach based on the policy of the forum, which qualifies as a nonmechanical approach. Neels *TSAR* 2010 671 at 672 argues that the incidental question may be governed by one of four possible legal systems namely the internal *lex fori*, the legal system indicated by the conflicts rules of the forum, the internal *lex causae* or the legal system referred to by the conflicts rules of the *lex causae*.

173. 2007 (1) SA 483 (C).

validity of the Dominican divorce orders. This matter constituted an incidental question, even though not recognized as such by the court. The court found that the validity of the defendant's divorce in the Dominican Republic had to be decided in terms of the rules of Australian private international law. In applying the Australian requirements for recognition of foreign divorce orders as contained in section 104(3) of the Australian Family Law Act of 1975, the court found that the divorce order was not valid and that the subsequent marriage in Australia between the plaintiff and defendant was therefore also invalid. The court therefore applied the legal system indicated by the rules of private international law of the *lex causae* to the incidental question.

§3. *Renvoi*

65. *Renvoi* refers to the situation where reference to a foreign *lex causae* in terms of the conflicts rules of the forum includes the conflicts rules of the *lex causae*, in other words, the reference is to the whole law of the *lex causae*, including its PIL.[174]

66. In terms of the partial-*renvoi* approach the foreign *lex causae* may then, in terms of its conflicts rules either refer the issue back to the forum or refer the issue to the law of a third country. However, when the issue is referred back to the forum or the law of a third country, the conflicts rules of the forum or the third country are not taken into account, in other words, the reference is to the internal law of the forum or the third country.

67. In terms of the foreign-court theory, the attitude or stance of the foreign *lex causae* towards *renvoi* must be considered. In other words, the forum has to place itself in the shoes of the foreign court, so to speak, and adopt the approach to *renvoi* that the foreign court would have adopted.

68. There is no authority on *renvoi* in South African PIL.[175] However, the application of *renvoi* has statutorily been excluded in two instances:

- *Renvoi* is excluded where domicile is the connecting factor: If a court, in the application of the choice-of-law rules, finds that a question before it should be decided in accordance with the law of a foreign state or territory on account of someone's domicile in that state or territory, the court shall decide that question in accordance with that law, even though a court of that state or territory, in the application of the choice-of-law rules, would have found the South African law or any other law to be applicable with respect to the question concerned;[176] or

174. See in general Edwards & Kahn *LAWSA: Conflict*, para. 286; Forsyth *Private International Law*, 91ff.
175. It seems that the partial-*renvoi* approach was adopted in *Ex Parte Low NO: In re Estate of Mangan*, 1915 SR 147.
176. Section 4 of the Domicile Act 3 of 1992. See also Neels 1992 *TSAR* 739.

– in regard to the formal validity of Wills section 3*bis* of the Wills Act[177] has been amended to refer, in all instances, to the internal law of foreign countries, thereby excluding any possibility of *renvoi* arising in this respect.

69. There seems to be consensus amongst commentators on South African PIL that *renvoi* is excluded in respect of international commercial contracts.[178]

§4. *ORDRE PUBLIC* (PUBLIC POLICY)

70. The forum may refuse to apply a foreign *lex causae* indicated by a particular multilateral conflicts rule on the basis that the foreign law is contrary to the public policy of the forum. It may be said that public policy operates generally as an overriding check upon the application of the rules of foreign legal systems in our courts.[179] However, the forum should not apply its internal public policy too stringently to conflicts cases.[180]

71. Examples of the exclusion of foreign law on the grounds of considerations of public policy include the non-enforcement of gambling contracts,[181] the non-recognition of polygamous and incestuous marriages, as well as marriages contracted without the necessary consent,[182] the non-recognition and non-enforcement of foreign judgments which are contrary to our public policy or foreign judgments obtained without due observance of the principles of natural justice,[183] as well as the non-enforcement of foreign penal and revenue laws.[184]

72. The position regarding polygamous marriages merits some discussion. In keeping with internal public policy,[185] foreign polygamous marriages (whether actually polygamous or merely potentially so) are not recognized in South Africa.[186] However, the Constitution and its inherent values changed matters. When interpreting the Bill of Rights, a court must promote the values that underlie an open and democratic society based on human dignity, equality and freedom. A number of

177. 7 of 1953.
178. Edwards & Kahn *LAWSA: Conflict*, para. 331; Forsyth *Private International Law*, 101; Kahn 1983 *ASSAL* 496; Van Rooyen *Kontrak*, 107 fn. 2; Wethmar-Lemmer 2008 *De Jure* 419 423.
179. *Sperling v. Sperling* 1975 (3) SA 707 (A) 722C–D. See, in general, Edwards & Kahn *LAWSA: Conflict*, para. 293; Forsyth *Private International Law*, 120ff; Hahlo & Kahn *Husband and Wife*, 583.
180. Forsyth *Private International Law*, 121–122; Hahlo & Kahn *Husband and Wife*, 583. See also Corbett, Hofmeyr, Kahn *Succession*, 611 where Kahn agrees that a foreign rule should be rejected on the grounds of public policy only if it flies 'in the face of some deep-rooted conception of good morals'.
181. *Timms v. Nicol* 1968 (1) SA 299 (R).
182. Edwards & Kahn *LAWSA: Conflict*, para. 293.
183. *Ibid.*
184. It may be argued that penal laws and revenue laws constitute a separate category in respect of the exclusion of the indicated foreign law, since the reasons for these exclusions may not necessarily be based on public policy. For a discussion of the rationale for these exclusions, see Forsyth *Private International Law*, 123–125.
185. *Ismail v. Ismail* 1983 (1) SA 1006 (A).
186. *Seedat's Executors v. The Master (Natal)* 1917 AD 302.

recent cases brought about changes in regard to the recognition of certain consequences of domestic polygamous unions. In *Ryland v. Edros*[187] it was decided that, in view of the values of equality and tolerance of diversity and the recognition of the pluralistic nature of South African society in the Constitution of the Republic of South Africa,[188] the enforcement of obligations from a Muslim marriage was in keeping with public policy and the *boni mores* of South African society. In *Amod v. Multilateral Motor Vehicle Accident Fund*,[189] Mrs. Amod, whose husband had been killed in a motor car accident, lodged a claim against the Accident Fund for damages for loss of support. The Supreme Court of Appeal found that the Accident Fund was indeed under a legal duty to compensate her for her loss. In *Daniels v. Campbell NO and Others*,[190] the Constitutional Court extended the meaning of 'spouse' in the Intestate Succession Act 81 of 1987, and 'survivor' in the Maintenance of Surviving Spouses Act 27 of 1990, to a wife or husband married in accordance with Muslim rites. The *Daniels* case concerned a de facto monogamous Muslim marriage. Justice Sachs acknowledged the transformation effected by South Africa's new constitutional order, which affirms the significance and equality of all South Africans and the constitutional goal of establishing a society based on democratic values, social justice and fundamental human rights. In *Hassam v. Jacobs NO and Others*[191] the meaning of 'spouse' in the Intestate Succession Act, and 'survivor' in the Maintenance of Surviving Spouses Act was further extended to include surviving partners to a polygamous Muslim marriage. Future PIL cases are likely to follow the same liberal approach. While the close identification between public policy in the international sense and internal public policy is generally not ideal, this area of the law only stands to benefit.

In *Burchell v. Anglin*[192] Crouse AJ made the following finding:

> [I]t is necessary to take moral values or public policy into consideration in the choice of law process. … In South Africa the highest test of public policy is our Constitution. Just as all South African law is under constitutional scrutiny, so any foreign law which a court intends to apply in South Africa should be placed under constitutional scrutiny. I must therefore also consider whether the law of Nebraska passes constitutional muster in South Africa before deciding I can apply same.[193]

In *Representative of Lloyds and Others v. Classic Sailing Adventures (Pty) Ltd*[194] the Supreme Court of Appeal recently stated obiter dictum that the values of the Constitution are norms of direct application.[195]

187. 1997 (2) SA 690 (C).
188. 108 of 1996.
189. 1999 (4) SA 1319 (SCA).
190. 2004 (7) BCLR 735 (CC); 2004 (5) SA 331 (CC).
191. 2008 (4) All SA 350 (C); 2009 (5) SA 572 (CC).
192. 2010 (3) SA 48 (ECG).
193. Paragraph 127.
194. 2010 (5) SA 90 (SCA).
195. Paragraph 25.

§5. Evasion of the Law

73. When a person performs an act in a foreign country with the intention to avoid the application of South African law, it is said that such a person has acted *in fraudem legis fori* and therefore the South African law, and not the normally applicable foreign law, will apply to the issue.[196]

74. The application of the *fraus legis* doctrine is most pronounced in family law, with specific reference to the essential validity of marriage.[197] The reason for this is that, unlike English law which uses *domicilium* as the connecting factor for essential validity, South African PIL has adopted the *lex loci celebrationis* as the applicable law for the essential validity of marriage.[198] This means that South African law (as the *lex domicilii*) may easily be evaded by marrying elsewhere and therefore there is a need for this exception to our general rule that the *lex loci celebrationis* determines the essential validity of marriage.[199]

75. Whether the *fraus legis* doctrine only operates in respect of the domestic law of the forum or whether it extends to the evasion of a foreign *lex causae* is an open question. Van Rooyen,[200] writing on contracts in South African PIL, argues that, by intentionally using a different connecting factor, the conflicts rules of the forum are evaded and therefore the *lex causae* that should have applied must apply, even though the legal system that was evaded is a foreign legal system and not the *lex fori*. In other words, the evasion was *fraus legis causae* (where the *lex causae* is a foreign legal system). Forsyth supports this view on the basis that its restriction goes contrary to the principle of the equality of legal systems, pointing out that, since *fraus legis* constitutes a separate ground of exclusion, it does not form part of the public-policy exclusion and, as such, has no special connection with the forum.[201]

§6. Proof of Foreign Law

76. In terms of South African common law, foreign law is regarded as a question of fact. This means that the party who seeks to rely on foreign law must both plead and prove it in court. This is done by means of evidence by an expert witness.[202]

---

196. See, in general, Edwards & Kahn *LAWSA: Conflict*, para. 295; Forsyth *Private International Law*, 126; Hahlo & Kahn *Husband and Wife*, 583.
197. *Ibid.*, See also *Kassim v. Ghumran* 1981 (4) SA 79 (Z).
198. *Friedman v. Friedman's Executors and Others* (1922) 43 NLR 259.
199. Schoeman 1992 (1) *Codicillus*, 22 at 27ff; Forsyth *Private International Law* 127. See further *infra* paras 170ff.
200. *Kontrak*, 173.
201. Forsyth *Private International Law*, 126.
202. On the common-law position, see Edwards & Kahn *LAWSA: Conflict* para. 288; Forsyth *Private International Law*, 107ff; Hahlo & Kahn *Husband and Wife*, 581ff.

77. This position changed when legislation was introduced in terms of which judicial notice may be taken of foreign law. In terms of the Law of Evidence Amendment Act[203] judicial notice may be taken of foreign law in so far as it may be readily ascertained with sufficient certainty.[204] While this does not preclude a party from pleading and proving a foreign legal rule in court,[205] it is no longer necessary to prove foreign law in every case.

---

203. 45 of 1988.

204. Section 1(1): see *Harnischfeger Corporation and Another v. Appleton and Another* 1993 (4) SA 479 (W); *Holz v. Harksen* 1995 (3) SA 521 (C); *C Hoare and Co. v. Runewitsch and Another* 1997 (1) SA 338 (W) for an application of this section. See also Forsyth *Private International Law*, 108; Kahn 1993 *ASSAL* 787ff; Kahn 1995 *ASSAL* 721. Section 9(1) of the proposed Application of Customary Law Bill of 1999 would have repealed s. 1 of the Law of Evidence Act 45 of 1988 but this initiative has now been overtaken by Project 90: Customary law.

205. Section 1(2).

Part II. Rules of Choice of Law

Chapter 1. Persons

§1. Natural Persons

78. The private-law status of natural persons is generally determined by their personal law, which, in the South African context, is the *lex domicilii.*[206]

I. Legal Capacity

79. Even though private-law status is determined by the *lex domicilii*, this does not mean that legal capacity is also necessarily determined by the *lex domicilii*. In this regard the distinction drawn by Huber between status and capacity, one of the incidents of status,[207] is significant for the conflict of laws. In terms of this distinction the status of the *propositus* (as determined by her personal law) follows her wherever she goes, but the capacities of such a status are determined by the law of the country where she wishes to exercise them.[208] In terms of this distinction between status and its resultant incidents the personal law determines a person's status, but not necessarily the incidents thereof.[209]

---

206. See in general De Winter 1969 III *Hague Recueil* 349 at 361–377; Edwards & Kahn *LAWSA: Conflict*, para. 296; Rabel *Conflict: Comparative*, 117ff; Spiro *Conflict*, 136ff; Yntema *Historic Bases*, 39ff.
207. For the distinction between status and its incidents, see Graveson *Conflict*, 230: 'Capacity or incapacity is merely one of the legally defined incidents of a legally imposed status. It differs from status in being merely part of a greater whole: in being the dynamic element of a static condition. While status is a legal condition, capacity is merely the sum total of powers attached by law, and not by act of the party, to that condition'.
208. See *De Conflictu Legum*, s. 12:
'Qualitates personales certo loco alicui jure impressas, ubique circumferri et personam comitari, cum hoc effectu, ut ubivis locorum eo jure, quo tales personae alibi gaudent vel subjecti sunt, fruantur et subjiciantur … ' translated thus in Lorenzen *Selected Articles*, 176: ' … personal qualities impressed upon a person by the law of a particular place surround and accompany him everywhere with this effect that everywhere persons enjoy and are subject to the law which persons of the same class enjoy and are subject to in that other place … ' S. 13 of *De Conflictu Legum* is to the same effect. See Suijling *Statuten-theorie*, 109–110 and Von Bar *Theory and Practice*, 38ff for a discussion of Huber's views, as well as Lorenzen *Selected Articles*, 136–180 for a comprehensive evaluation of Huber's *De Conflictu Legum*, as well as a translation thereof.
209. Falconbridge *Conflict*, 751ff; Graveson *Conflict*, 229ff; Allen 1930 *LQR* 277; Frames 1884 *Cape LJ* 253 at 301ff; Nygh 1961 *Tasm ULR* 555; Nygh 1964 *ICLQ* 39.

80. An example of an instance where the *lex domicilii* will probably not be decisive is contractual capacity, especially where a married woman may, in terms of her *lex domicilii*, have limited or no capacity to enter into a contract on her own. Therefore, when it comes to commercial contracts with third parties, a married woman should not be entitled to rely on contractual incapacity in terms of her domiciliary law (if such an incapacity exists) if she had contractual capacity according to the *lex loci contractus* or probably the putative proper law of the contract.[210] The reason for this is that it would be unfair to expect a third party to know where the woman is domiciled and furthermore, to know what her capacities are in terms of her *lex domicilii* if the domiciliary law is a foreign one. The same would presumably apply in the case of minors who also may have limited capacity to contract.

II. Name

81. The effect of marriage on the name of the wife is regarded as one of the personal consequences of marriage and, as such, it is governed by the *lex domicilii* of the parties at the relevant time.[211] It is uncertain whose domicile will be decisive should the parties have different domiciles; however, it is submitted that the *lex domicilii* of the wife should apply. National legislation regulates name changes in terms of the Births and Deaths Registration Act.[212]

III. Nationality

82. Nationality is not a common connecting factor in South African PIL, but where it is relevant, it will be determined with reference to the law of the country of which the person concerned is a citizen.[213] In terms of the South African Citizenship Act 88 of 1995, a child born in South Africa after 6 October 1995 as the child of South African citizens or permanent residents is a citizen of the Republic of South Africa, and a person born outside South Africa to a South African parent, is a South African citizen by descent upon registration of the birth under South African law. Citizenship may also be acquired through naturalization if certain conditions are met.[214]

---

210. Hahlo & Kahn *Husband and Wife*, 624. See also *Kent v. Salmon* 1910 TPD 637 in support of the *lex loci contractus*. Another case, *Powell v. Powell* 1953 (4) SA 380 (W), is susceptible to dissimilar interpretations. See further *infra* paras 111ff; Fredericks 2006 *THRHR* 279.
211. Hahlo & Kahn *Husband and Wife*, 622–623. On personal consequences of marriage, see further *infra* paras 195ff.
212. 51 of 1992.
213. Forsyth *Private International Law*, 50ff.
214. Section 4 of the South African Citizenship Act 88 of 1995.

IV. Change of Sex (Transsexuality)

83. Presumably a change of sex will be governed by the *lex domicilii* of the *propositus*, since this concerns his or her private-law status. However, there is no direct authority in South African PIL on this topic and it is submitted that the equality clause in the Constitution of the Republic of South Africa[215] gives a strong indication of the public policy of the forum in regard to the recognition of such a changed status.

§2. Legal Persons

84. Juristic persons (or artificial persons) include all entities which are not natural persons. The domicile or residence of these entities may be relevant for purposes of PIL, especially for founding jurisdiction. A corporation is notionally domiciled in the country in which it is incorporated (registered) and can only have one domicile. Therefore, it cannot acquire a second domicile if it trades in a country other than the one in which it is registered. The residence of a company is at its principal place of business or at the place of its registered office; so it is possible for a company to have more than one residence.[216]

85. Some uncertainty exists in regard to the residence of a foreign corporation operating in South Africa. It does not seem to suffice to register and establish a branch office in South Africa. The branch office must actively carry on the company's business.[217] If a foreign corporation does not have its principal place of business in South Africa, but does some business here, such residence will only be recognized 'in regard to a dispute which turns upon a cause of action arising out of the local business activities'.[218]

215. 108 of 1996 s. 9(3) and (4):

(3)The state may not unfairly discriminate directly or indirectly against anyone on one or more grounds, including race, gender, sex, pregnancy, marital status, ethnic or social origin, colour, sexual orientation, age disability, religion, conscience, belief, culture, language and birth.

(4)No person may unfairly discriminate directly or indirectly against anyone on one or more grounds in terms of subsection (3).

216. Edwards & Kahn *LAWSA: Conflict*, para. 304; Forsyth *Private International Law*, 211-212; *Bisonboard Ltd. v. K Braun Woodworking Machinery (Pty) Ltd.*, 1991 (1) SA 482 (A).

217. Harms *Civil Procedure* A4.12.

218. *ISM Inter Ltd. v. Maraldo and Another* 1983 (4) SA 112 (T) at 117B.

Chapter 2. Obligations

§1. Law of Contract[219]

I. Autonomy of the Parties (to Determine the Proper Law)

86. South African PIL recognizes the autonomy of the parties to determine the proper law of their contract. In other words, they are free to agree, either expressly or tacitly, on a specific legal system to govern their contract:

> That our law recognizes party autonomy in respect of the proper law of the contract seems clear. Thus where the parties have expressly or impliedly (or tacitly) agreed upon a governing law our Courts would give effect to the intention of the parties.[220]

87. Whether parties enjoy absolute freedom regarding their choice of legal system, is debatable. On the one hand it may be argued that they cannot, for instance, choose the legal system of a country that is in no way connected with the contract. On the other hand such a legal system (which has no actual link with the contract) may contain specialized rules pertaining to the subject-matter of the contract, for example a contract for the shipping of goods, and this may be the very reason why the parties chose that particular legal system as the proper law for their contract. There is no clear authority in South African PIL regarding possible limitations on the freedom of contracting parties to choose an applicable legal system.[221] Whether the parties may exclude, through their choice of a proper law, the *ius cogens* (mandatory rules) of a legal system otherwise closely linked to the contract, is an open question.[222] There is no clear authority and therefore this will have to be decided with reference to the common law, statutes or international conventions prevailing in that *rechtskring*.[223]

In a recent decision of the Supreme Court of Appeal concerning a dispute based on a marine insurance contract, the court was only willing to give effect to the choice of a foreign legal system as governing law insofar as the provisions of the

---

219. See in general Edwards & Kahn *LAWSA: Conflict*, paras 328–340; Forsyth *Private International Law*, 315ff; Van Rooyen *Kontrak*; Spiro *Conflict*, 155ff; Kahn 1990 *BML* (I) 203ff. For a comprehensive account of the history of the proper-law doctrine in South African law, see Edwards *Reception of 'Proper Law' Doctrine*, 38ff.
220. *Laconian Maritime Enterprise Ltd. v. Agromar Lineas Ltd.* 1986 (3) SA 509 (D & CLD) at 525F–G. See also *Standard Bank of South Africa Ltd. v. Efroiken and Newman* 1924 AD 171 at 186.
221. See Edwards & Kahn *LAWSA: Conflict*, para. 329; Forsyth *Private International Law*, 321ff; Van Rooyen *Kontrak*, 67ff.
222. See Forsyth *Private International Law*, 323–324, who supports a relatively wide concept of party autonomy, drawing attention to the distinction between international trade contracts (which should be subject to a wide concept of party autonomy, since contracting parties are, generally speaking, economically equal) and local contracts (where party autonomy should be limited, if necessary, to protect the economically weaker party).
223. *LAWSA: Conflict*, para. 461 especially fns 13–15.

foreign legislation were not in conflict with the relevant South African legislation.[224] The parties included a choice-of-law clause electing English law as the applicable law and the relevant provisions to be applied were contained in the English Marine Insurance Act of 1906. The relevant concomitant South African provisions in this regard are contained in the Short-term Insurance Act 53 of 1998. After conceding that the relevant provisions of the South African legislation 'are not prohibitory'[225] the court nevertheless found that the English Marine Insurance Act may not be applied insofar as it contains provisions in conflict with the South African legislation.[226]

88. Be that as it may, parties may choose a legal system as the proper law of their contract and this choice may be express or implied (tacit).[227]

A. *Express Choice of Law*

89. The most concrete expression of party autonomy is an express choice of law in a contract. Usually such an express choice can easily be identified, for example: 'This contract shall be governed by German law'.

B. *Implied (or Tacit) Choice of Law*

90. It is more problematic to infer a choice of law from the terms of a contract or to identify a tacit choice of law in a contract. It could be argued that if the contracting parties had agreed on an applicable legal system, they should have expressed themselves clearly on this point. However, it may also be argued that, by agreeing, for instance, on a specific country as the seat of arbitration in the event of a dispute arising, the parties had in fact agreed on the legal system of that country as the applicable law for their contract. This view is based on the maxim *qui elegit iudicem elegit ius* (he who chose the judge, chose the law).[228] In an English decision, *Tzortzis v. Monarch Line A/B*,[229] it was held that by exercising their choice to have London as the seat of arbitration, the parties tacitly chose English law as the applicable law. However, in a later case, *Compagnie d'Armement SA v. Compagnie Tunisienne de Navigation SA*,[230] the House of Lords held that the presence of an

224. *Representatives of Lloyds v. Classic Sailing Adventures (Pty) Ltd* 2010 (5) SA 90 (SCA).
225. Paragraph 22 of the decision.
226. Paragraph 29 of the decision. Forsyth *Private International Law* 321 argues that this decision does not negate the principle of party autonomy, since the court meant to refer to directly applicable statutes 'that override the choice-of-law process and apply irrespective of the proper law of the contract". On the other hand, Van Niekerk 2011 *TSAR* 159 170 comments that the court did follow an approach of "cutting down if not altogether ignoring a choice of foreign law clause'.
227. See Forsyth *Private International Law*, 325: 'A choice is none the less genuine for being made tacitly'.
228. Forsyth *Private International Law*, 328.
229. [1968] 1 All ER 949.
230. [1971] 1 AC 572.

arbitration clause in an international contract was not necessarily indicative of an implied choice of law. The latter English judgment was quoted with approval in the South African case of *Benidai Trading Co Ltd. v. Gouws and Gouws*:[231]

> [I]n the international commercial world it has almost become a universal practice to select London as the seat for arbitration proceedings, not because the parties to an international mercantile transaction necessarily have confidence in English law, but for purposes of convenience, because London is an important commercial centre and because of the expertise of London arbitrators ... Not only do the parties not submit to the jurisdiction of the English law, but, unless a clear inference is to be drawn to the contrary, they do not even accept English law as the proper law of the contract ... This was clearly held by the House of Lords in the matter of *Compagnie D'Armement Maritime SA v. Compagnie Tunisienne de Navigation SA.*[232]

91. Other examples of a tacit choice of law may include the use of technical terms from a specific legal system,[233] or reference to an Act of parliament of a specific country.[234] With regard to the latter, a caveat must be sounded, since parties may incorporate only certain statutory measures of a specific country in their contract, while the legal system of another country is in fact the proper law of the contract. Other *indicia* may also point to an implied or a tacit choice of the proper law, such as the form of the document used (e.g., a printed standard-form antenuptial contract);[235] the use of concepts or business jargon specific to certain trading activities; and so forth.[236] However, it must be remembered that these factors are mere indications of a tacit choice of law by the parties and therefore these *indicia* must have a reasonable connection with the contract to justify the inference of such a tacit choice.[237] Indeed it may be difficult to distinguish between a tacit choice of law and the absence of a choice of law.

231. 1977 (3) SA 1020 (T).
232. At 1028H–1029A.
233. Forsyth *Private International Law*, 328.
234. Compare *Stretton v. Union Steamship Company Ltd.* (1881) 1 EDC 315.
235. See *Ex Parte Spinazze and Another NNO*, 1985 (3) SA 650 (A) at 665F–H: '... the contract was in South African form; it was entered into in order to avoid a matrimonial property regime, viz. community of property, which obtained in South Africa at the time, but not in Italy ... at the time when the contract was executed the deceased was domiciled and resident in South Africa; and the parties to the contract obviously intended South Africa to be their matrimonial home and the country where the contract was to operate. These factors may be taken either as indicating a tacit choice of South African law, or, at any rate, as showing that South African law was the system with which the contract had its closest and most real connection'.
236. See Edwards & Kahn *LAWSA: Conflict*, para. 329 fn. 3.
237. Neels & Fredericks 2011 *De Jure* 101 discuss the requirements for a tacit choice of law in the draft Hague Principles on Choice of Law in International Contracts and refer to the fact that the relevant provision requires a tacit choice of law to 'appear clearly from the provisions of the contract or the circumstances' (at 109). See article 3 of the draft Hague Principles on Choice of Law in International Contracts, accessible at http://www.hcch.net/upload/wop/contents_rpt_june2011e.pdf.

II. No Choice of Law by the Parties

92. In the absence of an express or an implied choice of law by the parties, the proper law of the contract must be determined by the court.

93. In the past the *lex loci contractus* and the *lex loci solutionis* were regarded as important (or the sole) indicators of the proper law, in the absence of a choice of law by the parties.[238] However, not only may the place of contracting be fortuitous with no substantial links with the contract,[239] it may also be difficult to establish where the contract was concluded.[240]

94. Unlike the place of contracting, the place where performance must take place will seldom be merely fortuitous and thus a stronger case can be made for the *lex loci solutionis* to be the proper law of the contract. However, this solution is also fraught with difficulties, for example, where the parties have to perform in different places or even where the separate performances of one or both parties are to take place in different places.[241]

95. As a result of the unsuitability of the *lex loci contractus – lex loci solutionis* rule for modern times, different approaches to the determination of the proper law of the contract, in the absence of an express or tacit choice by the parties, have emerged.

96. The approach initially adopted by the South African courts was the so-called subjective approach[242] that presumes that the parties intended some legal system to apply to their contract. This approach was adopted by our then Court of Appeal in *Standard Bank of South Africa Ltd. v. Efroiken and Newman.*[243]

97. In terms of this subjective approach, which is also called the presumed intention theory, the court attempts to determine what the intention of the parties concerning the choice of a proper law would have been, had they applied their minds to the issue. In order for the court to assign or impute an intention to the parties, the court takes into account all relevant factors, such as: the place where the contract was concluded, the flag of a ship, the place where a company is registered, where the parties do business, where the parties are domiciled, where performance in terms of the contract has to take place, the seat of arbitration, etc.[244]

---

238. This was based on Roman-Dutch authority: see Edwards *Huldigingsbundel*, 40–41; Kahn 1990 *MBL*, (I) 203 at 204. See also *Standard Bank of South Africa Ltd. v. Efroiken and Newman* 1924 AD 171 at 185ff.
239. Forsyth *Private International Law*, 332.
240. For example, offer and acceptance through ordinary mail, or by way of the Internet.
241. Forsyth *Private International Law*, 333.
242. Dicey *Digest*, 540.
243. 1924 AD 171 at 185.
244. See further Edwards *Huldigingsbundel*, 53ff.

98. This approach was endorsed in subsequent cases.[245] It has not yet been expressly rejected by the Supreme Court of Appeal, despite the impossibility of determining what the actual, subjective intention of the parties was with regard to the choice of a proper law, because the parties did not apply their minds to the matter. The presumed intention will always remain a fiction. It is quite possible that the parties may, in reaction to the determination of the proper law of their contract by the court, argue that that was not what they had in mind. Also, a specific contract or aspect of a contract can only have one applicable law, so, logically speaking, only one intention can be imputed to the parties. In practice it may be possible to impute a different intention to each party and therefore the court will have to choose between the two. The factors, which the court takes into account in order to impute an intention to the parties, operate in an objective manner to localize the contract. As such, it may be asked whether the court does in fact impute an intention to the parties, or whether it merely utilizes this terminology to justify its mode of operation which rests upon the conviction that the parties enjoy absolute freedom of contracting and that the will (or intention) of the parties with regard to their contract should be given effect.[246] Ultimately, it may be argued that it does not make sense at all to attempt to impute an intention to the parties if they had not expressly chosen a proper law for their contract or if a tacit choice of a proper law cannot be inferred from the contract.

99. Despite the fact that the subjective approach has not yet been rejected by our highest court, there is a definite inclination towards the objective approach. The objective approach, which was first formulated by Westlake,[247] implies that the proper law of the contract is determined with reference to that legal system which has the closest and most real connection with the contract. This approach was adopted by the English courts, which initially had followed Dicey's subjective approach, after the judgment in *Bonython v. Commonwealth of Australia*:[248] 'The proper law of the contract is the system of law by reference to which the contract was made or that with which the contract has its closest and most real connection'.[249] Even though our Supreme Court of Appeal has not yet rejected the subjective approach adopted in the then Appeal Court case of *Standard Bank of South Africa Ltd. v. Efroiken and Newman*,[250] and judges consider themselves bound by the *Efroiken* case, but express support for this view in obiter dicta.[251] The objective

245. See especially *Guggenheim v. Rosenbaum (2)* 1961 (4) SA 21 (W) at 31A.
246. For further general criticism of the subjective approach, see also Edwards *Huldigingsbundel*, 54ff, 63; Kahn 1983 *ASSAL* 449; Van Rooyen *Kontrak*, 217.
247. *Treatise*, 258.
248. 1951 AC 201.
249. At 219. This was endorsed in *Amin Rasheed Shipping Corp v. Kuwait Insurance Co.* [1983] 2 All ER 884 (HL) at 887–888.
250. 1924 AD 171.
251. *Improvair (Cape) (Pty) Ltd. v. Establissements Neu* 1983 (2) SA 138 (C) at 146H–147A; *Laconian Maritime Enterprises Ltd. v. Agromar Lineas Ltd.* 1986 (3) SA 509 (D) at 526D–H and 530I; *Ex parte Spinazze* 1985 (3) SA 633 (A) at 665H. The latter is an interesting decision, which concerned the formal validity of an antenuptial contract and the court had to determine the proper law of the antenuptial contract. In deciding that the proper law of the antenuptial contract was South African law, Corbett J.A. said the following at 665F–H:

approach is jurisprudentially more sound than the subjective approach, since it does not seek to impute an intention to the parties, but rather to determine, objectively, which legal system has the closest and most real connection with the contract.

100. In order to determine the presumed intention of the parties, or, rather, which country's legal system has the closest and most real connection with the contract, the court may consider the following factors:

- the *locus solutionis*;
- the place where the contract was concluded;
- the place of the offer;
- the place of acceptance;
- the place of agreed arbitration;
- the choice of jurisdiction;
- the domiciles of the parties;
- the place where the parties carry on business;
- the domicile of agents or mandatories of the parties;
- the future domicile of the parties;
- the (habitual) residence of the parties;
- the nationality of the parties;
- the form, terminology and language of a contract; or
- the *locus rei sitae*, etc.[252]

However, it is not a mere process of localization of the contract. The court weighs the importance of every relevant factor; a single factor may indeed weigh more than three others together. In other words, the court must determine where the centre of gravity of the contract is. The evaluation is thus rather qualitative than quantitative, since the court determines the proper law of the contract by establishing which legal system has the most substantial connection with that contract.[253]

101. The most important factor to determine the proper law is the *locus solutionis*. The principle that can be deduced from the relevant South African case law is that the *lex loci solutionis* constitutes the proper law of the contract unless specific circumstances indicate another legal system. If the *locus solutionis* in respect

'... the contract was in South African form; it was entered into in order to avoid a matrimonial property regime, viz. community of property, which obtained in South Africa at the time, but not in Italy ... at the time when the contract was executed the deceased was domiciled and resident in South Africa; and the parties to the contract obviously intended South Africa to be their matrimonial home and the country where the contract was to operate. These factors may be taken either as indicating a tacit choice of South African law, or, at any rate, as showing that South African law was the system with which the contract had its closest and most real connection'. While not expressly rejecting the subjective approach adopted in *Standard Bank of South Africa Ltd. v. Efroiken and Newman*, this *dictum* may be seen as a clear vote for the objective approach.

252. Compare e.g., Fredericks & Neels 2003 *SA Merc LJ* 67–68; Neels and Fredericks 2008 *THRHR* 529.

253. *Laconian Maritime Enterprises v. Agromar Lineas* at 528G–H; *Kleinhans v. Parmalat* [2002] 9 BLLR 879 (LC) para. [21]; *Parry v. Astral Operations Ltd.* [2005] 10 BLLR 898 at para. 40; in general also Fredericks 2006 *SA Merc LJ* 80.

of the characteristic performance differs from the *locus solutionis* in respect of payment, two different options present themselves. Support for the 'one contract one proper law' approach is to be found in *Improvair (Cape) (Pty) Ltd. v. Establissements Neu.*[254] Support for the 'one contract, more than one proper law' approach is to be found in *Laconian Maritime Enterprises Ltd.*[255]

102. Ex parte Spinazze[256] constitutes a clear vote in favour of the objective approach. The case dealt with an antenuptial contract and not a commercial contract. Nonetheless, it is submitted that it should have persuasive authority for commercial contracts. Generally speaking, South African writers on the conflict of laws are also in favour of the objective approach.[257] Furthermore, it is submitted that the adoption of an objective formulation in the Rome I Regulation[258] could possibly serve as persuasive authority for South African courts.

III. Scope of the Proper Law

103. Once the proper law of a contract has been determined, it does not mean that the proper law governs all aspects of that contract. It would seem as if the proper law of the contract cannot be applied to those aspects of an international contract which relate to the coming into existence of the contract, since no contract is in existence yet.[259] In some of these instances, the 'putative' proper law may be invoked, in other words, that legal system which would have been the proper law had a valid contract come into existence.[260] However, as soon as a valid contract has come into existence, the proper law is available. Some of the more important aspects of international commercial contracts will now be addressed.

IV. Legal Form (Formal Validity) of a Contract

104. The formal validity of a contract dealing with immovable property will be determined with reference to the *lex rei sitae* or probably, alternatively, the *lex loci*

254. At 147F–G. Fredericks & Neels 2003 *SA Merc LJ* 71 and Fredericks 2006 *SA Merc LJ* 81 support this approach and propose that all the relevant factors must be considered. If the proper law is to be one of the *leges loci solutionis*, an ad hoc rule in favour of the *lex loci solutionis* in respect of payment should prevail. While this methodology was not expressly followed in *Kleinhans v. Parmalat SA (Pty) Ltd.*, [2002] 9 BLLR 879 (LC) at para. 105, the result was in accordance therewith.
255. At 528–529 and 530H–I. Forsyth *Private International Law*, 334 ascribes this view to a failure to understand the Copernican Revolution in conflict of laws and highlights the assumptions underlying the view of Fredericks & Neels.
256. 1985 (3) SA 633 (A).
257. Forsyth *Private International Law*, 329–330; Kahn *Appendix: Succession*, 623; Spiro *Conflict*, 159; Van Rooyen *Kontrak*, 217–218; Fredericks & Neels 2003 *SA Merc LJ* 66.
258. EC Regulation 593/2008 on the Law Applicable to Contractual Obligations (Rome I Regulation).
259. Compare Edwards *Huldigingsbundel*, 65.
260. Edwards & Kahn *LAWSA: Conflict*, para. 331.

contractus.[261] Regarding other contracts, it is submitted that their formal validity will be subjected to the requirements of the *lex loci contractus*.[262] However, the *lex loci contractus* is not without its problems. In the modern world, the place where a contract is concluded may be wholly unimportant, fortuitous or difficult to establish, since contracts may be concluded by letter, fax, telephone, electronically (for instance by e-mail) or on board an aeroplane or a vessel. Thus the proper law of the contract has also been mooted as an alternative legal system in terms of which the formal validity of a contract may be tested. This would amount to a facultative approach in terms of which the *lex loci contractus* and the proper law of the contract are stated in the alternative for formal validity.[263]

105. The facultative approach to formal validity was applied in a case concerning an antenuptial contract. In *Ex Parte Spinazze and Another NNO*[264] Corbett J.A. decided that the formal validity of an antenuptial contract, entered into in Italy, may be determined with reference to the *lex loci actus* or the proper law of the contract.[265] The facultative approach has found application in the context of commercial contracts in at least one instance.[266]

V. Validity, Formation of a Contract

106. To determine whether a contract has been formed, for instance whether an offer has been accepted, is problematic. As this issue pertains to the possible coming into existence of a contract, the proper law of the contract cannot be applied, since there is not, as yet, proof of the existence of the contract. The best solution to this dilemma would seem to be to apply the putative proper law, in other words, that legal system which would have been the proper law had the contract in fact come into being. Edwards and Kahn submit that the putative proper law should determine whether a contract has in fact been concluded, as well as whether an offer has been accepted.[267]

107. It is often necessary to determine whether one or both parties to a contract did in fact have the capacity to enter into that contract, for example a minor who enters into a contract without the consent of one of her parents or guardian. Since the issue of contractual capacity pertains to the coming into existence of the contract (there can be no contract if one or both parties lack contractual capacity), the proper law of the contract cannot be used to determine whether the parties had the capacity to enter into the contract. Where the parties did in fact choose the proper

261. See Van Rooyen *Kontrak*, 137ff, who bases his view on Roman-Dutch authority as well as case law: *Ferraz v. D'Inhaca* 1904 TH 137; *Hamburg v. Pickard* 1906 TS 1010 (PC); *Roux v. Kuils River Syndicate* 1912 TPD 547; *Consolidated Estates and Trusts Ltd. v. Turnbull* 1924 TPD 1.
262. Edwards & Kahn *LAWSA: Conflict*, para. 334.
263. Forsyth *Private International Law*, 341–343; Van Rooyen *Kontrak*, 141.
264. 1985 (3) SA 650 (A).
265. For a discussion of the *Spinazze* case, see Edwards 1986 *THRHR* 144; Spiro 1986 *THRHR* 139.
266. *Creutzburg & another v. Commercial Bank of Namibia Ltd.* [2006] 4 All SA 327 (SCA).
267. *LAWSA: Conflict*, para. 332 and authority cited there.

law to govern their contract, such choice would not necessarily be decisive, since it is unacceptable for parties to intentionally manipulate their choice of a particular legal system in order to gain the capacity to enter into a contract, which capacity they would not otherwise have had.[268]

108. There are four possible legal systems according to which contractual capacity may be tested, namely the *lex domicilii*, the *lex loci contractus* or the putative proper law and, in the event of a contract involving immovables, the *lex rei sitae*. A party may be incapable of entering into a contract in terms of her *lex domicilii*, but be able to do so in terms of the putative proper law of the contract. Since the position in South African PIL is not settled, the issue of contractual capacity merits some discussion.

109. As capacity is closely connected to private-law status, it is sometimes maintained that capacity, just like status itself, should be governed by the *lex domicilii*. However, if one analyses the position it becomes clear that capacity is but one of the incidents of status: when you have the status of a minor, one of the incidents of such status is that you cannot enter into a contract without the assistance of one of your parents or your guardian. Huber, in particular, drew a clear distinction between status and its incidents: Whereas status is governed by the *lex domicilii*, an incident such as capacity to contract is governed by the *lex loci actus*.[269] In terms of this distinction between status and its resultant incidents the personal law determines a person's status, but not necessarily the incidents thereof.[270] Several cases may be mentioned in this context.

110. In *Hulscher v. Voorschotkas voor Zuid-Afrika*,[271] a minor, unmarried woman, domiciled in Holland at that stage, borrowed money to emigrate to South Africa. When she was 21 years of age, she married Mr Hulscher. Mr Hulscher was subsequently sued for the debt owed by his wife when they were married. The magistrate rejected the defendant's plea that the contract his wife had entered into was invalid *ab initio* as she had been a minor at that stage. The defendant lodged an appeal. Innes C.J. scrutinized the authoritative sources regarding the question whether a minor's capacity to contract should be determined by the *lex domicilii* or

268. Edwards & Kahn *LAWSA: Conflict*, para. 333.

269. See *De Conflictu Legum*, s. 12:

'Qualitates personales certo loco alicui jure impressas, ubique circumferri et personam comitari, cum hoc effectu, ut ubivis locorum eo jure, quo tales personae alibi gaudent vel subjecti sunt, fruantur et subjiciantur … ' translated thus in Lorenzen *Selected Articles* 176: ' … personal qualities impressed upon a person by the law of a particular place surround and accompany him everywhere with this effect that everywhere persons enjoy and are subject to the law which persons of the same class enjoy and are subject to in that other place … ' S. 13 of *De Conflictu Legum* is to the same effect. See Suijling *Statuten-theorie*, 109–110 and Von Bar *Theory and Practice*, 38ff for a discussion of Huber's views, as well as Lorenzen *Selected Articles*, 136–180 for a comprehensive evaluation of Huber's *De Conflictu Legum*, as well as a translation thereof.

270. Falconbridge *Conflict*, 751ff; Graveson *Conflict*, 229ff; Allen 1930 *LQR* 277; Frames 1884 *Cape LJ* 253 at 301ff; Nygh 1961 *Tasm ULR* 555; Nygh 1964 *ICLQ* 39. See also the discussion *supra* paras 84ff.

271. 1908 TS 542.

the *lex loci contractus*, but found it unnecessary to make a choice between the two possibilities, because the *locus domicilii*, as well as the *locus contractus*, was Holland. Therefore, this case fails to provide any clarity on this point.

111. In *Kent v. Salmon*,[272] the contractual capacity of a married woman was in issue. Mrs. Kent had been married in England in community of property. She bought goods in the Transvaal (a former province in South Africa) without her husband's assistance. The storekeeper maintained that English law, namely the wife's *lex domicilii*, should apply in order to render her liable for the payment of the debt. (However, it would appear that Mrs. Kent's husband had been domiciled in the Transvaal at the time the disputed contract was entered into by his wife: in terms of the law pertaining to the then domicile of dependence of a married woman (now abolished by the Domicile Act)[273] Mrs. Kent was thus domiciled in the Transvaal.) Smith J. held, however, that even if England were to be regarded as Mrs. Kent's *locus domicilii*, the contractual capacity of a married woman must be determined by the *lex loci contractus* (i.e., Transvaal law). Thus it is evident that the judge definitely distinguished between status, which is governed by the *lex domicilii*, and one of its incidents, namely contractual capacity, which is governed by the *lex loci contractus*.

112. In *Powell v. Powell*[274] the parties were domiciled in England at the time of the marriage, but subsequently moved to South Africa where they acquired a domicile. The husband then gave a gift to his wife which he later wanted to revoke. However, in terms of English law such a gift was irrevocable, while, under Roman-Dutch law (prevailing in South Africa at the time the gift was made), spouses could not make valid donations to each other. Ludorf J. applied the *lex domicilii* at the time that the gift was made, in other words South African law. There are, however, indications that the judge applied the *lex domicilii* as the (putative) proper law of the contract.[275]

113. In *Tesoriero v. Bhyjo Investments Share Block (Pty) Ltd.*,[276] the court had to decide whether a married woman had the necessary capacity to enter into a suretyship agreement without her husband's consent, as the appellant raised the defence of lack of contractual capacity on the part of the appellant, who had been married in community of property in terms of Argentinean law. The court held that a deed of suretyship signed by one of two equal members of a trading close corporation, and who is involved in the appellant's business, constitutes an ordinary commercial contract. The judge remarked that the *lex loci contractus* and the *lex causae* (the proper law) coincided and proceeded to apply the South African law, regarded as being the only legal system the contract was connected to.[277] Scholars differ as to

272. 1910 TPD 637.
273. 3 of 1992.
274. 1953 (4) SA 380 (W).
275. See especially Van Rooyen *Kontrak*, 124. Fredericks 2006 *THRHR* 279 submits tentatively that the case constitutes authority for the *lex domicilii* approach.
276. 2000 (1) SA 167 (W).
277. At 172H.

whether the case should be taken as authority for the *lex loci contractus* or for the (objective putative) proper law.[278]

114. It would appear that the *lex rei sitae* will be applied in respect of contractual capacity pertaining to immovable property.[279] However, the *lex domicilii*, the *lex loci contractus* and the application of the putative proper law of the contract provide problems in regard to contractual capacity. For instance, the implication of allowing a minor to raise incapacity in terms of her *lex domicilii* as a defence, could be unfair as this would mean that storekeepers are expected to be aware of a minor's place of domicile. If the *locus contractus* is fortuitous it would be unfair to allow contractual capacity to be governed by it.[280]

115. Finally, reference may be made to some persuasive authority: In Scots law a distinction is drawn between commercial and non-commercial contracts. In the case of the former the *lex loci contractus* applies, whereas in regard to the latter, such as marriage contracts, the *lex domicilii* may play a role. It appears that the distinguishing factor is the involvement of third parties (apart from the spouses) in a contract.[281] Forsyth supports this proposition.[282]

VI. Performance of a Contract

116. Performance is generally governed by the proper law of the contract,[283] save for instances where the proper law may be excluded on the basis of the public policy of the forum or certain mandatory rules of relevant connected legal systems.[284] More particularly, the proper law of the contract will govern the substance of the parties' obligations, while the manner of performance will be governed by the *lex loci solutionis*.[285] The *lex loci solutionis* (the law of the place of payment) will also fix the currency in which payment must be made.[286]

278. See Fredericks 2006 *THRHR* 282–283.
279. *Ferraz v. D'Inhaca* 1904 TH 137 at 142–143.
280. See Edwards & Kahn *LAWSA: Conflict*, para. 333.
281. Anton *Private International Law*, 276–279.
282. *Private International Law*, 340-341. See however, Kahn 1991 *MBL* (V) 126 at 128 who suggests that a party should in general be held to have contractual capacity in respect of movables if she has capacity at the time of contracting in terms of her *lex domicilii* or the *lex loci contractus* or the putative proper law while, in regard to immovable property, all the testing laws regarding movable property apply with a fourth possibility, namely the *lex rei sitae*.
283. Edwards & Kahn *LAWSA: Conflict*, para. 338.
284. See *infra*.
285. Edwards & Kahn *LAWSA: Conflict*, para. 338.
286. Edwards & Kahn *LAWSA: Conflict*, para. 338 especially fn. 16; Van Rooyen *Kontrak*, 192ff.

VII. Breach of Contract (Including Damages)

117. Since breach of contract relates to the substance of the parties' obligations in terms of the contract, this should logically be governed by the proper law of the contract.[287] The quantum of damages will also be determined by the proper law.[288]

VIII. Rescission of a Contract

118. It is submitted that this aspect forms part of the substance of the contract and should be governed by the proper law of the contract.[289]

IX. Interpretation

119. Van Rooyen proposes that the proper law of the contract should be applied to the interpretation of the contract.[290]

X. Illegality

120. The legality of a contract is determined by the proper law of the contract.[291] Therefore, a contract which is illegal in terms of its proper law will not be enforced by the forum.[292]

121. A contract, though legal in terms of its proper law, may be refused enforcement due to illegality according to the statutory law of the forum. Forsyth points out that a rule of the *lex fori* which strikes down a contract (legal in terms of its proper law) must be interpreted carefully to ensure that it was indeed intended to override the choice-of-law process and apply to foreign contracts.[293] Edwards and Kahn cite foreign exchange regulations as an example in this context.[294]

122. A contract, valid under its proper law, may also be refused enforcement by the *lex fori* if it contravenes the public policy of the forum. This is the well-known exception of *ordre public*. However, a measure of uncertainty exists in respect of the ambit of the doctrine of public policy. It is impossible to predict with certainty which terms in an international contract will militate against South African public

287. See Edwards & Kahn *LAWSA: Conflict*, para. 339 especially fns 3–6, 8.
288. *Stewart v. Ryall* (1887) 5 SC 146; Van Rooyen *Kontrak*, 200ff.
289. See, in general, Van Rooyen *Kontrak*, 202ff.
290. *Kontrak*, 186ff. See also Edwards & Kahn *LAWSA: Conflict*, para. 335.
291. Edwards & Kahn *LAWSA: Conflict*, para. 337 especially fn. 1.
292. Edwards & Kahn *LAWSA: Conflict*, para. 337; Forsyth *Private International Law*, 344.
293. *Private International Law*, 344.
294. *LAWSA: Conflict*, para. 337 fn. 2.

policy. It is generally accepted that the doctrine of public policy should be restricted in the field of conflict of laws: thus public policy in international matters would not necessarily include everything embraced by the term 'public policy' as it pertains to a purely internal matter.[295]

123. Although illegality in terms of the *lex loci contractus* could possibly have played a role in the past, no compelling reasons exist in modern law for a contract to be struck down because it is illegal in terms of the *lex loci contractus.*[296]

124. The position regarding illegality in terms of the *lex loci solutionis* is more complicated. Edwards and Kahn suggest that the effect of illegality under the *lex loci solutionis* should be determined by the proper law of the contract. The proper law may, in such circumstances, excuse performance, or require a substituted performance or substituted place of performance.[297]

125. The question whether mandatory rules of a substantially connected legal system (also called a 'third country') can render an otherwise valid contract illegal and unenforceable, has not been settled in South African PIL. Forsyth is of the opinion that such a principle should not be created by judges or imposed by the legislator, since it would undermine legal certainty in international commercial contracts, frustrate the benefits of party autonomy, and cast doubt on the theoretical proposition that the reason why foreign law is applied is by the command of the local sovereign.[298] Van Rooyen seems to recognize the applicability of the mandatory rules of a third country.[299] Roodt is also of the view that an analysis of the nature, scope and purpose of particular rules – as the unilateralist method requires – could, in certain instances, be vital for a new conception of comity and the internationalization of choice of law. Since the local sovereign is responsible for promulgating rules that may determine when foreign law should be applied, this methodology does not threaten the power of the sovereign to ordain when foreign law should be applied.[300]

§2. Particular Contracts

126. The principles of South African PIL relating to international contracts are of general application; therefore particular contracts are not, as a rule, treated separately. However, there are a few statutory enactments that deserve attention either because they are of a mandatory nature or because they embody public policy. Some

---

295. Edwards & Kahn *LAWSA: Conflict*, para. 337 fn. 3; Van Rooyen *Kontrak*, 161ff. See also *Timms v. Nicol* 1968 (1) SA 299 (R).
296. Edwards & Kahn *LAWSA: Conflict*, para. 337.
297. *LAWSA: Conflict*, para. 337.
298. *Private International Law*, 345ff.
299. *Kontrak,* 164ff.
300. Roodt 2005 *TSAR* 706.

of these enactments concern the protection of the weaker contractual party, such as employees and consumers.

I. Employment Contracts

127. No multilateral conflicts rules exist for employment contracts. However, South African domestic labour legislation is applicable to anyone employed within the Republic of South Africa.[301]

Proposals for the development of the common law in respect of the place of work as a factor that determines jurisdiction have been made with reference to sections 8(3) and 39(2) of the Constitution.[302]

II. Insurance Contracts

128. No multilateral conflicts rules exist in this regard. Previously, section 63(1) of the Insurance Act[303] provided that the owner of a domestic policy was entitled to enforce his or her rights under the policy against any insurer in any South African court of competent jurisdiction and determined that any question of law arising from any such policy would be decided according to South African law. However, the Insurance Act was repealed recently and no conflict rule was included in the new insurance legislation.[304]

In *Representative of Lloyds v. Classic Sailing Adventures (Pty) Ltd*[305] sections 53 and 54 of the Short-term Insurance Act 53 of 1998 were found to be rules of immediate application that the parties could not contract out of by a choosing another legal system as the law applicable to their contract.[306] Section 53 concerns the effect of non-disclosure and misrepresentations on an insurance policy and section 54 concerns the validity of insurance contracts. The court found that an insured cannot waive the benefits under sections 53 and 54, since such a waiver would be contrary to public policy and that therefore, parties may also not contract out of such provisions.[307]

301. Labour Relations Act 66 of 1995; Basic Conditions of Employment Act 75 of 1997. In general *Kleinhans v. Parmalat SA (Pty) Ltd.* [2002] 9 BLLR 879 (LC); *Parry v. Astral Operations Ltd.* [2005] 10 BLLR 989 (C); (in *Astral Operations Ltd v. Parry* (2008) 29 ILJ 2668 (LAC) it was found that the Labour Court had no jurisdiction to entertain the claim) Roodt 2003 *SA Merc LJ* 135; Fredericks 2006 *SA Merc LJ* 75.
302. Calitz 2011 *Obiter* 678.
303. 27 of 1943.
304. See s. 73 of the Long-term Insurance Act 52 of 1998.
305. 2010 (5) SA 90 (SCA).
306. Paragraphs 24 and 25 of the decision. See Van Niekerk 2011 *TSAR* 159 for a detailed analysis of this case.
307. Paragraph 24 of the decision.

III. Carriage of Goods by Sea

129. The Carriage of Goods by Sea Act[308] stipulates that the Hague Rules[309] apply to carriage of goods by sea in ships where the port of shipment is a port in South Africa.[310]

IV. Transfer of Bills of Lading

130. For purposes of PIL, the Sea Transport Documents Act 65 of 2000 excludes the otherwise applicable legal system in favour of its own provisions. Section 2(1) of the Act provides that the provisions of the Act apply to any sea transport document issued in South Africa; to goods consigned to a destination in South Africa or landed, delivered or discharged in South Africa, and to any proceedings instituted in South Africa after the commencement of the Act in respect of any such document or goods.

V. Credit Agreements

131. No multilateral conflicts rules exist in this regard. In South African domestic law the National Credit Act[311] regulates credit agreements.

VI. Bills of Exchange

132. In terms of section 70(a) of the Bills of Exchange Act[312] the formal validity of a bill drawn in one country and negotiated, accepted or payable in another, is governed by the law of the place of issue and the formal validity of every supervening contract[313] is determined by the law of the place where the contract was made. However, a bill issued outside South Africa is not invalid because it is not stamped in accordance with the law of the place of issue[314] and a bill so issued which conforms in respect of formal requirements to South African law, may for purposes of enforcing payment thereof, be treated as valid between all persons who negotiate, hold or become parties to it in South Africa.[315]

---

308. 1 of 1986.
309. The rules are contained in the International Convention for the Unification of Certain Rules of Law Relating to Bills of Lading (Brussels, 1924) as amended by the Brussels Protocol (1968): see Schedule to the Act.
310. Section 1(1)(a).
311. 34 of 2005. The operation of the Act is phased in as from 1 Jun. 2006 to 1 Jun. 2007. This regulatory framework pulls together different types of creditors.
312. 34 of 1964.
313. For example, acceptance, endorsement or acceptance for *honour supra protest*.
314. Section 70(a)(i).
315. Section 70(a)(ii).

133. The interpretation of the contract of the drawer, endorser, acceptor or acceptor for *honour supra protest* is determined by the *lex loci contractus*, provided that, if an inland bill is endorsed outside South Africa, the endorsement must, as far as the payer is concerned, be interpreted in terms of South African law.[316]

134. The duties of the holder in respect of presentment for acceptance or payment, and the necessity for, or sufficiency of, a protest or notice of dishonour or otherwise, are governed by the law of the place where the act takes place or the bill is dishonoured.[317]

135. The Act further provides that, in respect of a bill drawn outside South Africa, but payable in South Africa, not expressed in South African currency, in the absence of an express stipulation to the contrary, the amount will be calculated in accordance with the rate of exchange for sight drafts at the place of payment on the day the bill is payable.[318]

136. Finally, the due date for a bill drawn in one country and payable in another is governed by the law of the place where it is payable.[319]

VII. Consumer Contracts

136.1. No multilateral conflicts rule exists in this regard. The Consumer Protection Act 68 of 2008 took effect on 31 March 2011. According to section 5(1)(a) of the Act, it applies to 'every (consumer) transaction occurring within the Republic', subject to a list of exceptions in sections 5(2)-(4). Section 5(8)(a) stipulates that the Act is applicable irrespective of whether the supplier resides or has its principal office outside or within the Republic.[320]

§3. Non-contractual Obligations

I. Law of Delict

137. Until recently, the issue of choice of law in respect of the law of delict was *res nova* in South Africa.[321] Academic opinion remains divided on whether the *lex*

316. Section 70(b).
317. Section 70(c).
318. Section 70(d).
319. Section 70(e).
320. See Neels 2010 *Obiter* 122 for a discussion of the Consumer Protection Act and its private international law implications.
321. Crawford 1968 *SALJ* 314 at 318–319; Du Plessis *Gedenkbundel*, 120; Edwards 1979 *SALJ* 48 at 51; Edwards *LAWSA: Conflict*, para. 473; Forsyth *Private International Law*, 350; Kahn 1950 *SALJ* 66 at 67; Terblanche 1997 *CILSA* 243. Cases which touched on the issue of international

fori, the proper law of the delict, or the *lex loci delicti commissi* should be applied to international delicts.[322]

This topic was adjudicated upon by the Eastern Cape High Court in 2010. The case of *Burchell v. Anglin*[323] concerned a cross-border defamation claim. The plaintiff, the proprietor of a game reserve and hunting safari business in South Africa, alleged that the defendant made defamatory statements about him to a booking agent in Nebraska, USA and this resulted in a substantial decrease in bookings and financial loss to the plaintiff. The question arose whether South African law or American law should be applied to the claim. The court found that the *lex loci delicti* was Nebraskan law (paragraph 118). However, Crouse AJ stated that 'doubt exists whether the application of a single formula, such as the *lex loci delicti*, leads to adequate results (paragraph 119) and questioned whether *lex loci delicti* is a sufficient test to achieve justice between the parties' (paragraph 120). Crouse argued that 'internationally, a balancing test is used to determine the jurisdiction with the most significant relationship to the parties and the delict, and then the law of that jurisdiction is applied' (paragraph 122). The court decided to follow this approach and found that Nebraskan law was the law of the most significant relationship to the parties and the delict (paragraph 125). The court found that Nebraskan law would have to pass constitutional muster before it could be applied (paragraph 127).

A. *Lex Fori*

138. Arguments in favour of the application of the *lex fori*, as the law of the forum where the action is brought, are based on the views of Von Savigny.[324] According to him there was a close relationship between criminal and delictual liability: since foreign law could not be applied in criminal matters, foreign law could also not be applied to settle delictual issues. Today, this argument can no longer be accepted, since delictual liability is regarded as an instrument of distributive rather than retributory (as in the case of punishment) justice.[325]

139. Von Savigny also argued that delictual liability was closely related to the public policy of the forum. However, there is no reason why delicts are more closely related to the forum than, for instance, contracts. Furthermore, it is undesirable to apply the *lex fori* to a set of facts which stands in a closer relationship to a legal system other than the *lex fori*, unless there is a local measure which aims to promote a specific moral or public interest – an 'overriding local statute'. However, according to Von Savigny, all measures concerning delicts fell into this category.[326]

---

delicts, but which are all inconclusive, are: *Mackay v. Philip* (1830) 1 Menz 455; *Rogaly v. General Imports (Pty) Ltd.* 1948 (1) SA 1216 (C); *Standard Chartered Bank of Canada v. Nedperm Bank Ltd.* 1994 (4) SA 747 (A); *Minister of Transport, Transkei v. Abdul* 1995 (1) SA 366 (N).

322. See Forsyth *Private International Law* 349ff.

323. 2010 (3) SA 48 (ECG). See also Schulze 2010 *Annual Survey* 179 for a discussion of the *Burchell*-case.

324. Von Savigny *Private International Law*, 253ff.

325. See Forsyth *Private International Law*, 352–353.

326. Savigny *Private International Law*, 253ff.

140. The *lex fori* approach may also be criticized on the grounds that it would encourage forum shopping (the search for the most advantageous *forum*). However, this may be countered by strict rules of jurisdiction. Von Savigny maintained that only the court of the place where the delict was committed and the court in whose area of jurisdiction the wrongdoer is domiciled will have jurisdiction.[327] Ehrenzweig,[328] a modern exponent of the *lex fori* approach, introduces the jurisdictionary rule of forum non conveniens in this context. He argues that application of the *lex fori* in fact means application of 'the law of the proper forum'. One may criticize this interpretation of the *lex fori* on the basis that it would appear erroneous to solve problems concerning choice-of-law issues by employing rules of jurisdiction.

141. This discussion of the *lex fori* approach makes it clear that it is, in fact, misleading to refer to the mere application of the *lex fori.* Almost all the proponents of the *lex fori* approach qualify it in some way or other, in order to avoid inequitable and undesired consequences.[329] However, the *lex fori* has lost ground worldwide as a possible *lex causae* for international delicts and therefore the chances of adopting this approach in South Africa are slim.

B. The Proper Law of the Delict

142. The proper law of the delict as a possible *lex causae* for international torts was first proposed by the English writer, Morris. In terms of this approach the legal system which, on policy grounds, seems to have the most significant connection with the chain of events, should be applied.[330] While this approach found favour with American judges,[331] it is criticized on the basis of the underlying uncertainty in deciding which legal system has the most significant connection with the delict.[332] The decision in *Burchell v. Anglin* may be seen as support for this approach.[333]

---

327. *Ibid.*
328. Ehrenzweig 1968 *ICLQ*, 1.
329. Compare Edwards 1979 *SALJ* 48 at 79:

 '[T]his prima facie rule [i.e. the application of the *lex fori*] should be displaced if the court is convinced from the pleadings that the foreign law on which the litigant relies has a closer relationship to the facts of the case and to the parties than has South African law. In its adjudication of this issue the court should then consider the underlying purpose of both the local and the foreign law. Factors relevant to such an inquiry would include: the domicile and nationality of the parties; the place where the act causing the injury occurred; the place where the injury ensued; the place where any relationship between the parties is centred'.
330. Morris *Conflict*, 386ff.
331. See especially *Babcock v. Jackson* 191 NE 2d 279 (1963), 2 Lloyd's Rep 286.
332. Forsyth *Private International Law*, 357. Kahn in Hahlo & Kahn *Union*, 751 supports the proper law approach.
333. 2010 (3) SA 48 (ECG). at para. 122.

C. Lex Loci Delicti Commissi

143. The application of the law of the place where the delict occurred, the *lex loci delicti commissi*, may be justified on a number of grounds. It is a normal incidence of the principle of territorial sovereignty that only the law of the place where an act was committed can determine its legal consequences. In accordance with the *obligatio* theory the wrongful act is the source of an *obligatio* which follows the wrongdoer wherever she may go, and the sole source of this *obligatio* is the law of the place where the act has been committed.[334] On the other hand, the vested-rights theory demands the recognition and enforcement of rights that have been acquired in terms of the law of another country.[335]

144. Points of criticism against the *lex loci delicti commissi* rule are well-known: The *locus delicti* may be purely fortuitous (e.g., in the case of an air disaster where an aeroplane plunges into the ocean somewhere); the *locus* itself may be uncertain (e.g., where a harmful product is manufactured in one country, sold in another and causes damage in a third); non-recognition of considerations such as the respective domiciles and places of residence of the plaintiff and the defendant, as well as of the type of delict committed, may have appalling and undesirable results; and, finally, dissimilar sets of facts are gathered under one umbrella.[336]

145. Despite all its inherent deficiencies the *lex loci delicti commissi* appears to be a very popular conflict rule. The proponents of this rule in South Africa are of the opinion that the *lex loci delicti commissi* would in most cases be reasonably certain and that it is preferable to make provision for exceptions to the rule. As a point of departure it is thus proposed that the *lex loci delicti commissi* should apply as a general rule for choice of law in this context, but that deviations from it should be allowed under circumstances where its application is manifestly inappropriate, for example, where the plaintiff and defendant have a common residence, domicile or nationality and some other link between them (such as travelling in the same vehicle).[337]

D. The Rome II Regulation

145.1. The *Burchell* decision cannot be seen as having cast a conflict rule in stone for the law of delict.[338] Mention may be made of the Rome II Regulation[339]

334. Edwards 1979 *SALJ* 48 at 55ff; Forsyth *Private International Law*, 353.
335. Edwards 1979 *SALJ* 55 fn. 88.
336. See, in general, Edwards 1979 *SALJ*, 48 at 56ff; Forsyth *Private International Law*, 353–355.
337. See Forsyth *Private International Law*, 355, as well as Du Plessis *Gedenkbundel*, 134, 138. See, however, Terblanche 1997 *CILSA* 243 at 262–263, who, on the basis of a comparative study, advocates a much stricter application of the *lex loci delicti commissi*. The *lex loci damni*, as it is applied in terms of Art. 4(1) of Rome II (Regulation (EC) No. 864/2007 of the European Parliament and of the Council on the law applicable to non-contractual obligations) is likely to feature if a comparative conflicts approach is followed by courts in South Africa.
338. Forsyth *Private International Law* 364.

which contains the conflict rules that apply to delict and other non-contractual obligations in the EU.

Article 4(1) of the Regulation expounds the general rule in respect of delict and determines that it shall be governed by 'the law of the country in which the damage occurs, irrespective of the country in which the event giving rise to the damage occurred and irrespective of the country or countries in which the indirect consequences of that event occur'. The general rule is therefore that the *lex damni* governs.[340] Article 4(2) provides that, 'where the person claimed to be liable and the person sustaining damage both have their habitual residence in the same country at the time when the damage occurs, the law of that country shall apply'. Article 4(3) directs that 'where it is clear from all the circumstances of the case that the tort/delict is manifestly more closely connected with another country, the law of that other country shall apply'. The challenge of the CJEU is to balance press freedom and personality rights in different circumstances, such as when content is placed online on an internet website. The *forum actoris* principle enables the plaintiff to institute action for the whole damage at the place where the victim of the infringements have the centre of his interests. In the majority of cases, this place would correspond with that person's habitual residence.

II. *Negotiorum Gestio*

146. There is no authority regarding choice of law pertaining to *negotiorum gestio* in South African PIL. Bennett[341] suggests that situations of *negotiorum gestio* differ considerably so that a single conflict rule is not desirable for the claims that may arise. The personal law of the principal or gestor could apply in instances where there is no prior arrangement between them but they share the same personal law and the transaction took place abroad. Where they did have a prior legal relationship, the law governing the prior contractual relationship is recommended. Where immovable property is involved, the *lex rei sitae* could provide the choice-of-law solution.

III. Unjustified Enrichment

147. There is no authority on choice of law regarding unjustified enrichment in South African PIL.[342]

339. Regulation (EC) 864/2007 of the European Parliament and Council on the Law Applicable to Non-contractual Obligations.
340. Forsyth *Private International Law* 362.
341. Bennet 1990 *ICLQ* 165–166.
342. For a comparative study of possible conflict rules for the solution of conflicts issues pertaining to unjust enrichment, see Bennet 1990 *ICLQ* 136. For an exposition of the basis of the South African law of unjust enrichment, see De Vos *Verrykingsaanspreeklikheid*. In general Forsyth *Private International Law* 365.

IV. Culpa in Contrahendo

147.1. There is currently no authority in respect of *culpa in contrahendo* in South African PIL. In all probability, the same South African PIL principles applicable to other delicts will be applied to *culpa in contrahendo*.

Chapter 3. Law of Property

§1. General Rules

I. *Lex Rei Sitae*

148. The *lex rei sitae* (the law of the place where the property is situated) determines whether property is movable or immovable.[343] An incorporeal right (such as a bond over immovable property) usually takes the classification of the object to which it pertains.[344]

II. Movables, Immovables

149. Most choice-of-law issues relating to property are dealt with in terms of the distinction between movable and immovable property.[345] Issues pertaining to immovable property are generally governed by the *lex situs*,[346] since the law of the place where such property is situated can deal effectively with it. Issues concerning movable property were traditionally referred to the *lex domicilii* in terms of the fiction *mobilia sequuntur personam*, which means that movables are situated where their owner is.[347] However, in modern times, the role of the *lex situs* in regard to movables has become more pronounced.[348]

III. Transfer of Property

150. In regard to movable property the fiction which underlies the maxim *mobilia sequuntur personam*, namely that a person's movables follow her wherever she goes, is not true in modern times. Therefore the *lex domicilii* of the owner can no longer be regarded as the basic conflicts rule for movable property. Not only is this rule based on a fiction, but it also fails to provide an answer when the very ownership of a movable is in issue, since the rule is based on the domiciliary law of the owner. In modern law the *lex situs* has taken over as the basic rule applicable to movables.[349] Apart from the inherent problems in applying the *lex domicilii* of the

343. Edwards & Kahn *LAWSA: Conflict*, para. 322; Forsyth *Private International Law*, 368.
344. This is not an absolute rule. Not every incorporeal right attached to immovable property is regarded as immovable. Certain leases are regarded as movable. Furthermore, bonds over immovable property may be regarded as movable in one *rechtskring* and as immovable in another *rechtskring*. See further Edwards *LAWSA: Conflict*, para. 322 fn. 2; Forsyth *Private International Law*, 368; Spiro *Conflict*, 57ff (who discusses Van der Keessel's views in this regard in great detail).
345. The conflict rule for proprietary consequences of marriage is an exception: both movable and immovable property are, as a single unit, subjected to the *lex domicilii matrimonii*: Hahlo & Kahn *Husband and Wife*, 630.
346. See Edwards & Kahn *LAWSA: Conflict*, para. 323.
347. Forsyth *Private International Law*, 371–372; Maasdorp's *Institutes*, 1.
348. See *infra* para. 150.
349. *Standard Bank of SA Ltd. v. Ocean Commodities Inc* 1983 (1) SA 276 (A) at 294D; *Marcard Stein and Co. v. Port Marine Contractors (Pty) Ltd.* 1995 (3) SA 663 (A) at 671H–J.

owner, application of the *lex situs* accords better with the expectations of the parties.[350] It is submitted that the *lex situs* will also govern issues concerning the capacity to acquire movables as well as the formal and essential validity of a transfer.[351] However, regarding a general transfer of movables (*titulo universali*), situated in different places, the *lex domicilii* will still apply in order to avoid the application of different *leges rei sitae* to the same estate, for example, upon death.[352] Also, in regard to matrimonial property, movables and immovables are regarded as a single unit and governed by the *lex domicilii matrimonii.*[353]

151. All aspects regarding the transfer of immovable property are governed by the *lex rei sitae*, since the forum of the *lex rei sitae* has effective jurisdiction over immovable property.[354] However, as far as matrimonial property is concerned, movables and immovables are treated as a single unit and as such are governed by the *lex domicilii matrimonii.*[355]

§2. Special Rules

I. Goods during Transit

152. While goods are in transit, the *lex rei sitae* does not present itself as a viable conflicts rule, since the very *situs* of the goods is unknown. South African courts have not pronounced on the question of which legal system governs goods in transit, so the issue is *res nova*. The *lex situs*, proper law, *lex domicilii* and *lex loci actus* are generally rejected.[356] Authorities support the *lex loci expeditionis* (the law of the place of dispatch) above the *lex loci destinationis*, since the place of dispatch is certain and definitely linked to the goods which were dispatched, whereas the destination may be uncertain or never reached.[357] Edwards and Kahn propose that 'the law of the country accommodating the seat of the juristic act' should determine the substantive validity and legal consequences of the transaction; however, they also submit that there cannot be a single rule to govern all the different instances of goods in transit.[358] The commercial practice of transferring goods by means of documents of title may explain the lack of authority on this point. Since there is no relevant ascertainable court to which this matter can be referred, the forum is likely to apply its own law.

350. See Edwards & Kahn *LAWSA: Conflict*, para. 324; Forsyth *Private International Law*, 372.
351. Edwards & Kahn *LAWSA: Conflict*, para. 324; Forsyth *Private International Law*, 346–347 (who seems to be of the opinion that the *lex loci actus* may also be applied to test formal validity).
352. Edwards & Kahn *LAWSA: Conflict*, paras 318–321.
353. Hahlo & Kahn *Husband and Wife*, 630.
354. Edwards & Kahn *LAWSA: Conflict*, para. 323; Forsyth *Private International Law*, 370–371.
355. Hahlo & Kahn *Husband and Wife*, 630.
356. Forsyth *Private International Law*, 375; Neels 1991 *TSAR* 309 at 315.
357. 1991 *TSAR* 309 at 316–318. Forsyth *Private International Law*, 376 supports this view except where the *res in transitu* ceases to be such. However, he points out that the *lex loci expeditionis* can never be an absolute rule, since the law of the flag of a ship may play a role in respect of the validity of the transfer of the vessel's bunker oil while it is on the high seas.
358. Edwards & Kahn *LAWSA: Conflict*, para. 456 fn. 12.

II. Securities (for a Debt)

153. According to South African case law hypothecation over both movable and immovable property is governed by the *lex rei sitae*.[359]

III. Mortgage

154. Mortgage bonds registered over land have been classified as movable[360] or immovable[361] in South African law. In *Lief NO v. Dettmann*[362] this varying classification was confirmed:

> [T]he determining factor in classifying a mortgage bond either as immovable or movable for any particular purpose, may, generally speaking, be said to depend on whether the purpose in question relates more particularly to the bond as constituting an acknowledgement of debt or as an instrument of title to a real right in the land hypothecated thereby.[363]

155. Forsyth suggests that classification of the mortgage bond should take place in accordance with the *lex rei sitae* of the *res* to which it pertains (not the *lex rei sitae* of the mortgage bond).[364]

IV. Pledge

156. It is submitted that pledge is governed by the *lex rei sitae* of the *res*.[365]

V. Cession

157. A right of action is not attached to a *res* and therefore there is no *lex rei sitae* of a *res* available in this instance. When a right of action is ceded, the *lex loci actus* will govern the formal validity of the cession, while the *lex domicilii* of the debtor will govern the intrinsic validity.[366]

---

359. See Forsyth *Private International Law*, 377 and authority cited there.
360. *Reinhardt v. Ricker and David* 1905 TS 179 at 186.
361. *Union Government v. Fischer's Executrix* 1921 TPD 328.
362. 1964 (2) SA 252 (A).
363. At 266A.
364. *Private International Law*, 376.
365. Forsyth *Private International Law*, 377.
366. See Edwards & Kahn *LAWSA: Conflict*, para. 324 especially fn. 17; Forsyth *Private International Law*, 378.

Chapter 4. Intangible Property Rights

§1. Patent Law

158. In South Africa the Patents Act[367] governs all aspects relating to patent law. In particular, it provides that an application accompanied by a complete specification may claim priority from the date of an application in a convention country[368] relating to the same subject matter,[369] provided that the application in the convention country was lodged not earlier than one year before the convention application and was the first application in any convention country in respect of the relevant invention and that the applicant in the application claiming priority is the proprietor of the application in the convention country or the applicant has acquired the right to claim priority in South Africa.[370]

159. The Act further provides that where, after the lodging of the first application in a convention country in respect of any invention a subsequent application is lodged in that country in respect of the same invention, such subsequent application shall be deemed to be the first application in that country in respect of that invention if, at the time of the lodging thereof, the previous application had been withdrawn, abandoned or refused without having been open to public inspection; no priority rights have been claimed on the strength of such previous application and no rights are outstanding in the convention country in question in connection with such previous application.[371] An application which has been withdrawn, abandoned or refused will not, after lodging of a subsequent application relating to the same subject-matter, be capable of supporting a claim for priority rights in terms of the Act unless any rights are outstanding in South Africa or in any convention country in connection with the first-mentioned application.[372] Where a person has applied for protection for any invention by an application which, in terms of a treaty subsisting between any two or more convention countries, is equivalent to an application duly made in any one of those convention countries or in accordance with the law of any convention country, is equivalent to an application made in that convention country, he will be deemed to have applied in a convention country for purposes of the Act.[373]

367. 57 of 1978.
368. Any country, including any group of countries and any territory for whose international relations another country is responsible, which the South African President has, with a view to the fulfilment of any treaty, convention, arrangement or engagement, declared to be a convention country: see s. 2 of the Act.
369. Section 31(1)(c).
370. Section 31(1)(c)(iii)–(iv).
371. Section 31(2)(a)–(c).
372. Section 31(3).
373. Section 31(4)(a)–(b).

§2. COPYRIGHT

160. By its nature copyright protection is territorial.[374] In South Africa copyright is governed by the Copyright Act.[375] This Act provides that the Minister of Trade and Industry may by notice in the *Government Gazette* provide that any provision of the Act specified in the notice will in respect of any country so specified apply in relation to literary, musical or artistic works, computer programs, cinematograph films, sound recordings and published editions first published in that country as it applies in relation to the works just mentioned first published in South Africa; in relation to persons who at any material time are citizens or subjects of that country as it applies in relation to persons who at such a time are South African citizens; in relation to persons who at a material time are domiciled or resident in that country as it applies in relation to persons who at such a time are domiciled or resident in South Africa; in relation to bodies incorporated under the laws of that country as it applies in relation to bodies incorporated under South African law; in relation to broadcasts made and programme-carrying signals emitted to a satellite from places in that country as it applies in relation to broadcasts made and programme-carrying signals emitted to a satellite from a place in South Africa.[376] In terms of section 37(3) the Minister of Trade and Industry may not issue a notice in terms of this Act in respect of any country which is not party to a convention relating to copyright to which South Africa is also a party, unless the Minister is satisfied that, in respect of the class of works to which the notice relates, provision has been or will be made under the laws of that country whereby adequate protection will be given to the owners of copyright in terms of the Act.

---

374. Visser 1999 *SA Merc LJ*, 268.
375. 98 of 1978.
376. Section 37(1)(a)–(e).

Chapter 5. Company Law

161. In South African law companies are governed by the Companies Act[377] and the common law. No specific PIL rules exist in regard to companies; however, the Act contains certain provisions relating to external companies, in other words, companies or other associations accorded incorporated status in another country.[378] When an external company establishes a place of business in South Africa or engages in a transaction in South Africa its existence becomes relevant for purposes of South African company law. On the basis of reciprocity and in accordance with the international comity of nations, a body which enjoys corporate status in another country is accorded the same status in South Africa and domestic legislation provides for proper control over foreign incorporated bodies which operate in South Africa.[379]

377. 71 of 2008 (date of commencement 1 May 2011).
378. Section 1.
379. Section 23.

Chapter 6. Family Law

§1. Engagement and Extra-Marital Cohabitation

162. The only case of note concerning engagement in South African PIL was *Guggenheim v. Rosenbaum (2).*[380] In this case there was a breach of an agreement to marry and the court had to determine which legal system governed the contract of engagement. Trollip J. regarded the engagement as an ordinary commercial contract and sought to determine the proper law of the contract on the basis of the

> [L]aw of the country which the parties have agreed or intended or are presumed to have intended shall govern it; and in the case of a contract concluded in one country to be performed in another, then in the absence of an express term or any other indication to the contrary, it can be presumed that the proper law is the law of the latter (*lex loci solutionis*).[381]

This dictum embraces the subjective approach to the determination of the proper law of a contract in the absence of a choice (express of implied) by the parties and also reveals a preference for the *lex loci contractus – lex loci solutionis* approach. It is submitted that the objective approach in terms of which the legal system with which the contract has the closest and most real connection, will be the proper law, is preferable to the subjective approach adopted in *Guggenheim.*[382]

163. This dictum in *Guggenheim* thus leaves us with two possibilities, namely the proper law of the contract, as well as the *lex loci contractus – lex loci solutionis* approach. In the context of an engagement the determination of the proper law of the contract will proceed with reference to the centre of the social relationship between the parties at the time of the engagement, while the *locus solutionis* will in reality be the intended matrimonial domicile of the parties.[383] There are, however, also other *leges causae* available, such as the *lex fori*, the law of the place where the breach occurred and the personal law of either the plaintiff or the defendant.[384] Regarding the validity of an engagement, it has been suggested that the legal system or systems which govern the formal and intrinsic validity of marriage should also apply to engagements.[385]

164. As far as damages for breach of promise in regard to engagements are concerned, the usual principles in respect of contractual damages will apply. However, if an *iniuria* is involved, damages in this regard will be determined according to the principles of the law of delict.[386]

---

380. 1961 (4) SA 21 (W).
381. At 31A.
382. In regard to the proper law of the contract, as well as the *lex loci contractus – lex loci solutionis* approach, see *supra* paras 94ff.
383. See also Forsyth *Private International Law*, 279.
384. Spiro *Conflict*, 131.
385. Hahlo & Kahn *Husband and Wife*, 584.
386. Hahlo & Kahn *Husband and Wife*, 585.

165. There are no special PIL rules regarding extra-marital cohabitation. In the absence of definite authority it is submitted that the conflict rules for international contracts will govern any contractual extra-marital arrangements.

§2. MARRIAGE

166. The conception of a monogamous marriage as being the only 'civilized' form of union between life partners is no longer an accurate description in the South African context. Customary law permits polygamy. The Recognition of Customary Marriages Act[387] not only recognizes the validity of existing polygamous unions, but it also does not prohibit future unions of this nature, provided that the court has approved a written contract in which the future matrimonial property system of each union is set out.[388] Many domestic changes have taken place on account of sections 9(3) and (4) of the Constitution. Obligations arising from a potentially polygamous, yet de facto monogamous, union were recognized in *Ryland v. Edros*,[389] *Amod v. Multilateral Motor Vehicle Accident Fund*[390] and *Daniels v. Campbell NO and Others*[391] and obligations arising from a polygamous union were recognized in *Hassam v. Jacobs NO and Others.*[392] On the international level, the old policy of non-recognition of polygamous marriages is likely to undergo similar change.

I. Same-Sex Marriages

167. The equality clause embodied in Chapter 2 section 9 of the Constitution of the Republic of South Africa 108 of 1996, provides that neither the state nor a person may unfairly discriminate directly or indirectly against anyone on the ground of sexual orientation.[393] In the light of this clause, the common law definition of a marriage as a union between a man and a woman has been found to constitute an impediment to marriages between people of the same sex in *Minister of Home Affairs v. Fourie.*[394] This Constitutional Court ruling imposed a deadline to make same-sex marriages legal before 1 December 2006, and this led to the enactment of the Civil Union Act 17 of 2006, which took effect on 30 November 2006.

---

387. 120 of 1988.
388. Section 2(3).
389. 1997 (2) SA 690 (C).
390. 1999 (4) SA 1319 (SCA).
391. 2004 (7) BCLR 735 (CC); 2004 (5) SA 331 (CC).
392. 2009 (5) SA 572 (CC).
393. Section 9(3) and (4) provides:

    (3)The state may not unfairly discriminate directly or indirectly against anyone on one or more grounds, including race, gender, sex, pregnancy, marital status, ethnic or social origin, colour, sexual orientation, age disability, religion, conscience, belief, culture, language and birth.

    (4)No person may unfairly discriminate directly or indirectly against anyone on one or more grounds in terms of subsection (3).
394. *Minister of Home Affairs v. Fourie and others; Lesbian & Gay Equality Project and 18 others v. Minister of Home Affairs* 2006 (1) SA 524 (CC).

II. Validity of Marriage (Capacity, Form)

168. Both formal and essential (material or intrinsic) validity (which includes capacity) of marriage are governed by the *lex loci celebrationis* (the law of the place where the marriage was entered into).[395]

169. Regarding formal validity, there is one exception to the general application of the *lex loci celebrationis*. In terms of section 10 of the Marriage Act[396] a marriage solemnized in a country other than South Africa will be valid in South Africa if it was solemnized by a person appointed as a South African marriage officer in that country (e.g., persons in the consular or diplomatic services), provided that both parties to the marriage are South African citizens and domiciled in South Africa, and that the marriage was solemnized in accordance with the requirements set out in the Act. Such a marriage will be deemed to have been solemnized in the province of the Republic of South Africa where the husband is domiciled at the time. However, there is no legislation in South Africa which provides for the opposite scenario, namely where a marriage is solemnized in the South African consulate or embassy of a foreign country in accordance with the legal requirements of that foreign legal system. The formal validity of such a marriage will, in a South African court, be determined by the *lex loci celebrationis*, which will be South African law.[397]

170. Intrinsic validity concerns matters such as capacity, parental consent, degrees of blood relationship, etc. There are two exceptions to the general rule that the intrinsic validity of marriage is governed by the *lex loci celebrationis*. The first exception deals with the *fraus legis* doctrine. In terms of this doctrine the essential validity of a marriage will not be subjected to the *lex loci celebrationis* if the parties entered into marriage in another country with the intention to evade a local impediment to their marriage. Provided that at least one of the parties is domiciled in South Africa, the essential validity of such a marriage will, in a South African forum, be tested in terms of South African law. The doctrine applies only to *fraus legis fori*, that is where the forum is also the domicile of at least one of the parties.[398] Whether the *fraus legis* doctrine also pertains to formal validity, in other words, where parties have their marriage solemnized in another country to evade local formalities is uncertain. However, as Kahn points out, there seems to be little justification to extend this doctrine to formal validity in modern times. Formal requirements of such a mandatory nature will probably be enforced by the forum in terms of an overriding local statute.[399] The second exception pertains to the public policy of the forum (*ordre public*). Examples of marriages which will be invalid on the grounds

395. *Friedman v. Friedman's Executors and Others* (1922) 43 NLR 259; *Ochberg v. Ochberg's Estate* 1941 CPD 15. See also Schoeman 1992 (1) *Codicillus*, 22.
396. 25 of 1961.
397. See *Santos v. Santos* 1987 (4) SA 150 (W).
398. *Pretorius v. Pretorius* 1948 (4) SA 144 (O); *Kassim v. Ghumran and Another* 1981 (4) SA 79 (Z). See further Edwards & Kahn *LAWSA: Conflict*, para. 307; Forsyth *Private International Law*, 286-287; Hahlo & Kahn *Husband and Wife*, 596–597.
399. Hahlo & Kahn *Husband and Wife*, 596; 597 especially fn. 153.

of public policy, though valid in terms of a foreign *lex loci celebrationis*, are incestuous marriages or marriages entered into without having obtained the necessary parental consent.[400] Since the Constitution shapes the development of the common law, it remains uncertain whether the adherents of religious family laws enjoy unconditional constitutional protection regardless of the form and content of their marriage in the case of polygamous marriages. Whereas customary unions are covered by legislation,[401] the issue could remain grey, at an internal law level, if polygamous marriages concluded in South Africa or abroad in accordance with the Muslim faith are not openly recognized by legislation.[402] In the recent case of *AS v. CS*,[403] the *lex loci celebrationis* was also applied to determine the intrinsic validity of a foreign civil partnership.[404]

For purposes of international cases, public policy will be informed by the constitutional provisions of tolerance and equality.[405] It has been suggested that public policy be concretized in a legislative provision to the effect that a marriage entered into outside South Africa between parties, neither of whom is already married, is not void under the law of South Africa on the ground of having been entered into under a law that permits polygamy. The scope of application of this proposed rule ought to be clarified, so that it does not affect the determination of the validity of a marriage in accordance with the rules of private international law.[406]

III. Dissolution

A. *Annulment*[407]

171. In South African law a marriage may be annulled either because it was void *ab initio* or because it is voidable. A marriage is void *ab initio*,[408] for example, for failure to comply with certain prescribed formalities;[409] where one or both of the parties were already married by civil or African customary law; where one or both

400. Edwards & Kahn *LAWSA: Conflict*, para. 307. See also *Seedat's Executors v. The Master (Natal)* 1917 AD 302 at 307; Forsyth *Private International Law*, 288.
401. Section 10 of the Recognition of Customary Marriages Act 120 of 1998.
402. In 2010 the first version of the Draft Muslim Marriages Bill was published. It emanated from an investigation conducted by the South African Law Reform Commission on Islamic Marriages and Related Matters (Project 59). The Bill aims to provide a statutory framework for the recognition of Muslim marriages and their consequences. Several rounds of public comments were invited and amendments were made to the Bill. The Bill has provoked much public debate. It has not yet been enacted.
403. 2011 (2) SA 360 (WCC).
404. Paragraph 41 of the decision.
405. Forsyth *Private International Law*, 290.
406. Roodt 2008 *International Journal of Diversity*, 137.
407. For a detailed discussion of the grounds of jurisdiction and choice-of-law issues, see Schoeman *Domicile*, 54ff.
408. For a comprehensive list of the defects which will render a marriage null and void, see Sinclair *Law of Marriage*, 387ff.
409. See Sinclair *Law of Marriage*, 387–388 for a list of those formal defects which will render a marriage null and void. Failure to register a marriage will, for example, not have this effect: Sinclair *Law of Marriage*, 388.

of the parties were below the marriageable age;[410] where consent was lacking if the afflicted party (in the event of insanity or intoxication) was incapable of understanding the nature of the ceremony;[411] where the parties were within the prohibited degrees of blood relationship. In the past, the Prohibition of Mixed Marriages Act 55 of 1949 also rendered void marriages that took place across the colour line.[412] A marriage is voidable,[413] for example, if one of the parties was a minor and his or her parents had not consented to the marriage; if one of the spouses was impotent; if one of the parties was coerced into the marriage or if the wife was pregnant with the child of someone other than her husband at the time of the marriage. Strictly speaking, a marriage which is void *ab initio* need not be annulled in a court of law, and yet an annulment is often sought in order to clarify the status of the parties. However, the annulment of a void marriage does not alter the status of the parties: since the marriage was void *ab initio* the parties never acquired marital status and therefore such an annulment is in the nature of a declaration of an existing fact.[414]

172. The choice-of-law issue does not present serious problems in the case of the annulment of a void marriage. Since the grounds for annulment of a void marriage coincide with the requirements for a valid marriage, the question for the conflicts lawyer is simply whether a valid marriage came into being or not in the case of a failure to comply with certain prescribed formalities[415] or where the parties were within the prohibited degrees of blood relationship or where one of the parties was already married.[416] Therefore the South African conflict rule for validity, in terms of which the validity of a marriage is governed by the *lex loci celebrationis*, will be applied.[417]

173. However, in regard to the annulment of voidable marriages, there is no authority in South African law. Since the annulment of a voidable marriage alters the status of the parties, the matter should, in terms of the status theory,[418] be referred to the *lex domicilii.*[419] However, where domicile is the connecting factor and the parties have different domiciles at the time of the commencement of the suit,[420] it will have to be decided whose domicile is decisive. There are various

---

410. 18 years for boys and 15 years for girls.
411. However, the marriage may be validated if the parties continue to live together after the incapacity ceased to operate; alternatively, the marriage may be voidable: Sinclair *Law of Marriage*, 389.
412. This Act has since been repealed by the Immorality and Prohibition of Mixed Marriages Amendment Act 72 of 1985.
413. See Sinclair *Law of Marriage*, 387ff for a list of defects that will render a marriage voidable.
414. Hahlo & Kahn *Husband and Wife*, 559ff; Pollak *Jurisdiction*, 181ff.
415. See Sinclair *Law of Marriage*, 387–388.
416. For a comprehensive list of all the impediments that will render a marriage void *ab initio*, see Sinclair *Law of Marriage*, 387–390.
417. Hahlo & Kahn *Husband and Wife*, 641.
418. See in general De Winter 1969 III *Hague Recueil*, 349 at 361–377; Rabel *Conflict: Comparative*, 117ff; Spiro *Conflict*, 136ff; Yntema *Historic Bases*, 39ff.
419. See Hahlo & Kahn *Husband and Wife*, 641. Domicile is the only ground for jurisdiction regarding voidable marriages, so this will amount to the application of the *lex fori qua lex domicilii*. Forsyth, *Private International Law*, 311 argues in support of the *lex loci celebrationis*.
420. In terms of s. 1(1) of the Domicile Act 3 of 1992 a wife can acquire her own domicile, independent from that of her husband.

options in this regard. In matters of consent, there is the option to apply the *lex domicilii* of the person whose consent is allegedly defective.[421] In matters of incapability, there is the option of the domiciliary law of the person alleged to be incapable.[422]

B. Divorce

174. Section 2(1) and (3) of the Divorce Act[423] provide that:

(1) A court shall have jurisdiction in a divorce action if the parties are or either of the parties is:
   - domiciled in the area of jurisdiction of the court on the date on which the action is instituted; or
   - ordinarily resident in the area of jurisdiction of the court on the said date and have or has been ordinarily resident in the Republic for a period of not less than one year immediately prior to this date.

(2) A court which has jurisdiction in terms of this section in a case where the parties are or either of the parties is not domiciled in the Republic shall determine any issue in accordance with the law which would have been applicable had the parties been domiciled in the area of jurisdiction of the court concerned on the date on which the divorce action was instituted.

175. In terms of the above section the *lex fori* will govern all divorce issues, based on a fictional domicile in terms of section 2(3).[424] Since the choice-of-law aspect has been included in the section of the Divorce Act which deals with jurisdiction, it is clear that no proper distinction is drawn between jurisdiction and choice of law. The introduction of a 'fictional domicile' creates the impression that an attempt was made to remain true to the status theory in terms of which the *lex domicilii* determines status, or any change in status.[425] However, not only is it now possible to establish jurisdiction in a division of the High Court where none of the parties is domiciled (since jurisdiction may also be based on ordinary residence),[426] but the law applied to the divorce issue is to be the law of the fictional domicile which simply serves to indicate the *lex fori*. Therefore, a court other than the court of the domicile can assume jurisdiction and, as a result of this, a law other than the law of the domicile may be applied.

---

421. *Cheshire-North* (13th edn), 781.
422. *Cheshire-North* (13th edn), 785. See also Pålsson *Marriage and Divorce*, 314–315 for a discussion of the policy of validation in regard to the annulment of a marriage.
423. 70 of 1979.
424. For a historical account of jurisdiction and choice of law in regard to divorce, see Schoeman 1995 *THRHR* 488; Schoeman 1998 (4) *Fundamina*, 1.
425. See in general De Winter 1969 III *Hague Recueil*, 349 at 361–377; Rabel *Conflict: Comparative*, 117ff; Spiro *Conflict*, 136ff; Yntema *Historic Bases*, 39ff.
426. Section 2(1) of the Divorce Act 70 of 1979.

176. A closer look at section 2(3) of the Divorce Act[427] reveals that any issue relating to a divorce will be determined in accordance with the law that would have been applicable had the parties been domiciled in the area of the court's jurisdiction on the date that the action was instituted. 'Any issue' includes aspects such as the grounds of divorce,[428] as well as ancillary claims, such as maintenance and custody as well as, according to Kahn,[429] property rights which are not directly associated with the matrimonial property regime of the parties, for instance, forfeiture of the patrimonial benefits of the marriage in terms of section 9(1) of the Divorce Act.[430]

IV. Legal Effects of Marriage

177. The most important legal effect of marriage is that the private-law status of the parties changes to that of married persons. Previously the wife also acquired the domicile of her husband upon marriage, but this domicile of dependence has now been abolished by the Domicile Act.[431]

V. Matrimonial Property

178. In South African PIL proprietary consequences of marriage, in the absence of an antenuptial contract indicating a different legal system, are governed by the *lex domicilii matrimonii.*[432] Proprietary consequences include all issues pertaining to the estate(s) of the parties. These would primarily include the following: whether matrimonial property is held in or out of community of property or whether a partial community of property regime applies; the law governing the joint or separate estates of the spouses; the law governing antenuptial and postnuptial contracts;[433] the effect on the matrimonial property when the union is terminated through death

427. 70 of 1979.
428. *Gilbert v. Gilbert* (1901) 22 NLR 201; *Holland v. Holland* 1973 (1) SA 897 (T).
429. See 1979 *ASSAL* 496.
430. 70 of 1979.
431. 3 of 1992 s. 1(1).
432. The Roman-Dutch authorities are not entirely clear on this issue, partly because the *locus celebrationis* and the *locus matrimonii domicilii* very often coincided: see Hahlo & Kahn *Husband and Wife*, 627. After a thorough analysis of the old authorities in *Frankel's Estate v. The Master* 1950 (1) SA 220 (A) (see especially Van den Heever J.A.'s judgment at 240ff) it was decided that the *lex domicilii matrimonii* governed the proprietary consequences of marriage. See also earlier cases such as *Blatchford v. Blatchford's Executors* (1881) 1 EDC 365; *Brown v. Brown* 1921 AD 478; *Anderson v. The Master and Others*, 1949 (4) SA 660 (E); as well as subsequent affirmations of the rule in *Sperling v. Sperling* 1975 (3) SA 707 (A); *Milbourn v. Milbourn* 1987 (3) SA 62 (W); *Bell v. Bell* 1991 (4) SA 195 (W); *Esterhuizen v. Esterhuizen* 1999 (1) SA 492 (C); *Sadiku v. Sadiku* unreported, case no. 30498/06 (TPD). See also Edwards & Kahn *LAWSA: Conflict*, para. 309; Forsyth *Private International Law*, 295ff; Roodt 1995 *THRHR* 194; 440.
433. Whether a postnuptial contract may be entered into seems to be governed by the *lex domicilii* of the spouses at the time of the execution of such a contract: see Forsyth *Private International Law*, 299. It is not clear, however, whose domicile will be decisive should the spouses have different domiciles. See also *infra* paras 218ff.

or divorce as well as any other issue strictly related to proprietary consequences and the estate(s) of the parties.[434]

179. The matrimonial domicile (*domicilium matrimonii*) refers to the domicile of the husband at the time of marriage.[435] While this law may be more favourable to the wife than the law of her own domicile at the time of the marriage, the rule discriminates unfairly and finds no justification in terms of the principle of gender equality embodied in section 9 of the Constitution of the Republic of South Africa.[436] Moreover, the wife's domicile of dependence was statutorily abolished by section 1(1) of the Domicile Act.[437] Therefore, the jurisprudential basis for interpreting *domicilium matrimonii* as the domicile of the husband at the time of marriage has fallen away. However, the South African Law Commission, in the same report in which the abolition of the wife's domicile of dependence was announced, elected to retain the *domicilium matrimonii* as the connecting factor for proprietary consequences and, more importantly, reaffirmed the interpretation of the matrimonial domicile as the husband's domicile at the time of marriage.[438] It has also been questioned in case law whether the current connecting factor would pass constitutional muster.[439] Academic authors indicated that law reform with regard to the connecting factor is urgently needed,[440] and several proposals for two-step and three-step models have been made.[441] The constitution is likely to drive the reform of this common law conflicts rule in South African law.[442]

180. South African PIL adheres to the doctrine of immutability. In terms of this doctrine the matrimonial domicile (the domicile of the husband at the time of marriage) is fixed and remains fixed even if the parties subsequently acquire a new

---

434. Hahlo & Kahn *Husband and Wife*, 623; Edwards & Kahn *LAWSA: Conflict*, para. 309; Forsyth *Private International Law*, 295ff.

435. South African Law Commission: Working Paper 20 (Project 60) para. 6.7.

436. 108 of 1996. s. 9(3) and (4) read as follows:

(3) The state may not unfairly discriminate directly or indirectly against anyone on one or more grounds, including race, gender, sex, pregnancy, marital status, ethnic or social origin, colour, sexual orientation, age, disability, religion, conscience, belief, culture, language, and birth.

(4) No person may unfairly discriminate directly or indirectly against anyone on one or more grounds in terms of subsection (3). National legislation must be enacted to prevent or prohibit unfair discrimination.

In regard to the constitutional protection pertaining to gender equality, see, in general, Sinclair *Law of Marriage*, 66ff.

437. 3 of 1992 s. 1(1).

438. Report on Domicile 1990 (Project 60) paras 6.2–6.8, especially para. 6.7:

'The Commission ... decided not to recommend any statutory provision but to retain the common law rule in this regard. In the result the patrimonial consequences of marriage are still governed by the law of the place where the husband is domiciled at the time of marriage'.

439. *Sadiku v. Sadiku* unreported Case No. 30498/06 (TPD) (para. 10); *AS v. CS* 2011 (2) SA 360 371 (para. 55).

440. See especially Stoll & Visser 1989 *De Jure*, 330, as well as Forsyth *Private International Law*, 259 fn. 126; Neels 1992 *TSAR* 336–337; Visser 1995 *THRHR* 702–707; Van Schalkwyk 1999 *TSAR* 378–379; Neels 2003 *SALJ* 886 fn. 26; Roodt, *THRHR* 221 fn. 31, Neels & Wethmar-Lemmer 2008 *TSAR* 587.

441. Schoeman 2001 *TSAR* 72; Schoeman 2004 *IPRAX* 65; Schoeman 2004 *TSAR* 116–117.

442. Roodt 2006 *THRHR* 555.

domicile. The *ratio* for this doctrine is to protect the wife so that the husband cannot change the proprietary consequences of their marriage by changing his domicile.[443] The Appellate Division rejected the doctrine of the intended matrimonial domicile (when parties intend to assume a new domicile after marriage and want that domicile to be regarded as their matrimonial domicile) in *Frankel's Estate and Another v. The Master and Another.*[444] If parties wish for a legal system other than their actual *lex domicilii matrimonii* to govern the proprietary consequences of their marriage, they should express their wish in an antenuptial contract.

181. In terms of South African domestic law, parties may, upon joint application to a court that has jurisdiction in the matter, change their matrimonial property regime after marriage, provided that they comply with the requirements of the Matrimonial Property Act:[445] A husband and a wife, whether married before or after the commencement of this Act, may jointly apply to a court for leave to change the matrimonial property system which applies to their marriage, and the court may order that such matrimonial property system shall no longer apply to their marriage and authorize them to enter into a notarial contract by which their future matrimonial property system is regulated on such conditions as the court may think fit, provided it is satisfied that:

- there are sound reasons for the proposed change;
- sufficient notice of the proposed change has been given to all the creditors of the spouses; and
- no other person will be prejudiced by the proposed change.[446]

182. Whether this section allows for the postnuptial alteration of matrimonial property regimes in respect of marriages which are governed by a foreign legal system (in terms of the *lex domicilii matrimonii*) which does not provide for postnuptial contracts, is uncertain. While it is clear that section 21(1) was enacted for domestic marriages, Forsyth seems to be of the opinion that the section may apply to such 'foreign-law marriages', regardless of whether the foreign *lex domicilii matrimonii* permits postnuptial alteration or not. Since the consent of both parties is required (they must apply jointly) for such postnuptial alteration, there is no danger of one of the spouses being prejudiced. Also, the interests of third parties will be taken into consideration.[447]

183. The fact that the matrimonial domicile is fixed once and for all does not mean that the law of the matrimonial domicile is fixed as well. In an Appellate Division case, *Sperling v. Sperling*,[448] the law of the matrimonial domicile (the then East

443. *Brown v. Brown* 1921 AD 478 at 482. See also Edwards & Kahn *LAWSA: Conflict*, para. 309 n. 12; Hahlo & Kahn *Husband and Wife*, 631 especially fn. 463; Forsyth *Private International Law*, 298–299.
444. 1950 (1) SA 220 (A).
445. 88 of 1984.
446. Section 21(1).
447. Forsyth *Private International Law*, 299–300.
448. 1975 (3) SA 707 (A).

Germany) had changed retrospectively in regard to the matrimonial property regime of the parties concerned. The legal issue was whether the retrospective legislation should apply in the instant case, since the change in the *lex causae* took place after the parties had already acquired a new domicile in South Africa. Corbett J.A. applied the changed law of the *lex causae* on the basis of the balance of justice and convenience in the absence of any principle of public policy that militated against the application of the new law.

184. Movable and immovable property are regarded as a single unit for purposes of proprietary consequences of marriage. This means that, unless the parties have concluded an antenuptial contract and have chosen another legal system to govern their proprietary consequences, movable and immovable property, whenever acquired, are governed by the *lex domicilii matrimonii*.[449]

A. *Conflict between the Categories of Divorce and Proprietary Consequences*

185. It is often difficult to demarcate the boundaries of proprietary consequences accurately and precisely so as to draw a watertight distinction between the categories of proprietary consequences and divorce. Since divorce issues are governed by the *lex fori* in South African PIL,[450] and proprietary consequences by the *lex domicilii matrimonii*, the classification of an issue into either the category of proprietary consequences or the category of divorce may be crucial for the parties concerned, since different *leges causae* will determine the outcome of the case, depending on the category selected.

186. An issue that has specifically created difficulties for South African PIL in this regard is the question of redistribution of assets upon divorce. Section 7(3) of the Divorce Act grants the high court the entitlement to redistribute the assets of the spouses to be divorced.[451] This section provides that a court granting a decree of divorce in respect of a marriage out of community of property entered into before the commencement of the Matrimonial Property Act, 1984, in terms of an antenuptial contract by which community of property, community of profit and loss and accrual sharing in any form are excluded may on application by one of the parties to that marriage, in the absence of any agreement between them regarding the division of assets, order that such assets, or such part of the assets, of the other party as the court may deem just be transferred to the first-mentioned party.

187. Since the legislature does not seem to have borne in mind implications based on private international law when reforming certain aspects of the Divorce Act,[452] uncertainty exists with regard to whether section 7(3) of the Divorce Act is intended to apply to foreign marriages, and if so, how the judicial discretion to effect

449. Edwards & Kahn *LAWSA: Conflict*, para. 309; Hahlo & Kahn *Husband and Wife*, 629ff.
450. *Holland v. Holland* 1973 (1) SA 897 (T); s. 2(3) of the Divorce Act 70 of 1979: see *supra* paras 177ff.
451. 70 of 1979.
452. 70 of 1979.

a redistribution is supposed to be classified.[453] In a number of relevant cases, the issue of classification was not addressed consciously. Different outcomes resulted, depending on whether redistribution was treated as belonging to the category of divorce, the patrimonial consequences of marriage, or to both divorce and patrimonial consequences of marriage.

188. The view that the redistribution discretion belongs to the category of divorce and should be governed by the *lex fori*[454] was adopted in two different instances. In *Milbourn v. Milbourn*[455] the parties were domiciled in England at the time of marriage. They were married out of community of property by operation of law; in other words, they did not enter into an antenuptial contract. Upon divorce in South Africa the plaintiff sought a redistribution of assets on the basis of section 7(3) of the South African Divorce Act.[456] It was clear that, in terms of the South African conflict rule, the proprietary consequences of the marriage were governed by English law (as the *lex domicilii matrimonii*). The fact that the plaintiff attempted to invoke section 7(3) implies that the redistribution of assets was regarded as a divorce issue, governed by the *lex fori* in terms of South African private international law, which, in this particular case, was South African law. The plaintiff did not succeed, since the requirements of section 7(3), more particularly the existence of an antenuptial contract, were not met. In *Lagesse v. Lagesse*,[457] the *lex domicilii matrimonii* was the law of Mauritius. Nonetheless, section 7(3) was applied to effect a redistribution of assets, which implies that the issue of redistribution of assets was classified as a divorce issue, rather than as pertaining to proprietary consequences.

189. The view that the redistribution discretion belongs to the category of patrimonial consequences of marriage[458] was adopted in other instances, the first one of which shares the exact same fact scenario in *Milbourn v. Milbourn*. In *Bell v. Bell*,[459] the *lex domicilii matrimonii* was also English law and the parties were married out of community of property by operation of law. When their marriage ended in divorce in South Africa, the plaintiff did not rely on section 7(3) of the South African Divorce Act[460] for a redistribution of assets, but instead based her claim on sections 23 and 24 of the English Matrimonial Causes Act[461] and succeeded. Therefore, in this case, redistribution of assets was regarded as pertaining to the category

453. See Roodt 1995 *THRHR* 194; 440 on the classification problems which beset matrimonial property law.
454. Authors who wrote in support of this view include Kahn, 1991 *ASSAL* 585, Forsyth *Private International Law*, 309–310 and Van Schalkwyk 1999 *TSAR* 378.
455. 1987 (3) SA 62 (W): see Boberg 1987 *BML* 80; Kahn 1991 *ASSAL* 580–585; Lupton 1987 *BML* 119; Roodt 1988 *De Rebus* 59; Forsyth *Private International Law*, 308.
456. 70 of 1979.
457. 1992 (1) SA 173 (D): see Neels 1992 *TSAR* 336; Vrancken 1993 *TSAR* 180; Forsyth *Private International Law*, 308-309.
458. Heaton & Schoeman, 2000 *THRHR* 141 support this view; Schoeman 2001 *TSAR* 80.
459. 1991 (4) SA 195 (W): see Kahn 1991 *ASSAL* 580–586; Neels 1992 *TSAR* 336; Forsyth *Private International Law*, 309.
460. 70 of 1979.
461. 1973.

of proprietary consequences, and not divorce. In *Haines v. Haines*,[462] the plaintiff relied on the relevant provisions of the Matrimonial Causes Act of 1973 but later introduced a prayer in the alternative based on section 7(7) of the Divorce Act. The application to amend was refused on the basis of the *Milbourn* case, but the court also applied the law of the matrimonial domicile, referring to the *Bell* case with approval. In *Hassan v. Hassan*,[463] the judge classified the claim for redistribution on divorce as part of the patrimonial consequences of marriage and applied the Family Law (Scotland) Act of 1985. The court held that the *lex domicilii matrimonii* should govern both the patrimonial and maintenance aspects of the legislation in question, as both of these aspects were found to be highly interrelated and should not be separated.

190. The view that there are aspects of the redistribution discretion that are governed by the *lex fori* and aspects that are governed by the *lex domicilii matrimonii*[464] found support in the latest reported case, *Esterhuizen v. Esterhuizen.*[465] The applicability of section 7(3) to marriages of which the proprietary consequences are governed by a foreign *lex causae*, was again considered. In this case the *lex domicilii matrimonii* was the law of Namibia, which law did not allow for a redistribution discretion on the part of the courts. The parties entered into an antenuptial contract by means of which their marriage was in community of property in terms of Namibian law. The contract did not contain a choice-of-law clause in favour of South African law. The parties subsequently acquired a domicile in South Africa and upon divorce in a South African court, the plaintiff sought a redistribution of assets in terms of section 7(3). In this case it was decided that redistribution of assets belonged to the proprietary consequences of marriage (which was governed by Namibian law) and therefore section 7(3) could not be invoked for this purpose in terms of South African private international law.[466] This could be taken to imply that redistribution of assets was classified as a proprietary consequence and not as a divorce issue. Josman A.J. also concluded that, because the conflict rules provide that post-divorce maintenance is a divorce issue governed by the *lex fori*, the court could make a distribution order in terms of section 7(3) in respect of a foreign marriage to the extent that the order provides for a spouse's maintenance needs.[467]

191. Divergent categorizations of the discretion to redistribute assets may result in what is known as 'gap' ('*Normenmangel*' in German) in private international law. For example, in the *Bell* case,[468] both South African and English law provided for redistribution of assets on divorce which is a means of achieving a particular social

---

462. Unreported, Case No. 1683/1991.
463. 1998 (2) SA 589(D).
464. Neels 1992 *TSAR* 336; Neels 1993–2000, 10; Neels 2001–2002, 9; Neels 2001 *TSAR* 689. He refers in this regard to the interpretation given to s. 7(3) in domestic cases, at 698.
465. 1999 (1) SA 492 (C). See Heaton & Schoeman 2000 *THRHR* 148.
466. At 504C.
467. At 499, 504 it is clear that the court accepted Neels's argument as set forth in Neels 1992 *TSAR*, 336 in this respect. Heaton & Schoeman 2000 *THRHR* 148 disagrees with this aspect of the decision.
468. See discussion *supra*.

aim, namely fairness in property allocation upon divorce. However, section 7(3) of the South African Divorce Act[469] required an antenuptial contract and since the plaintiff and her husband were married out of community of property by operation of (English) law (and, therefore, did not enter into an antenuptial contract) the plaintiff could not rely on this section. By classifying the issue as part of the category of proprietary consequences, the plaintiff successfully relied on sections 23 and 24 of the English Matrimonial Causes Act.[470] However, as Kahn has pointed out, sections 23 and 24 of the English Act deal with the position of the parties *as from divorce* and therefore do not strictly pertain to proprietary consequences as such.[471] It is clear that the judge realized that he was faced with the problem of 'gap' in this instance:

> [A] person in the plaintiff's position would not enjoy her rights under the English law and would simultaneously be disbarred from enjoying her rights under the South African law'.[472]

Neels illustrates, with reference to *Hassan v. Hassan*[473] that *lex causae* classification leads to a total gap in both a formal and a material sense. He argues that reasonableness, simplicity, the clean-break principle and international harmony of decision support the application of Scottish law in that instance.[474]

192. Forsyth seems to support the decision in *Bell v. Bell*[475] on the basis that when a judge is confronted with the problem of 'gap', he or she should make an informed choice and that is, according to him, what happened in *Bell.*[476] Kahn is critical of the judge's resort to English law on the basis of having classified the redistribution of assets upon divorce as a proprietary consequence of marriage in *Bell*:

> [O]ne may doubt whether it justifies a characterization that does not really meet the test enunciated by Booysen J. in *Laconian Maritime Enterprises Ltd. v. Agromar Lineas Ltd.*, 1986 (3) SA 509 (D), which refers to 'sufficient evidence of the true nature of the foreign rule and its classification by its law … placed before the forum to enable it to make a correct classification of the rule according to the *lex fori*' (at 520H–I).[477]

Neels suggests that the claimant ought to be able to choose to litigate on the basis of section 7(3), which would apply if the redistribution discretion is viewed as a divorce issue, and section 7(9), which would apply if the redistribution discretion is

469. 70 of 1979.
470. 1973.
471. 1991 *ASSAL* 580–587.
472. 1991 (4) SA 195 (W) 199J–200A.
473. 1998 (2) SA 589 (D) 589.
474. Neels 2003 *SALJ* 892ff.
475. 1991 (4) SA 195 (W): see discussion *supra*.
476. *Private International Law*, 309–310.
477. 1991 *ASSAL* 580–588.

viewed as a patrimonial consequence of the marriage.[478] It would seem that section 7(9) implies that redistribution of assets should be regarded as being part of the proprietary consequences of the marriage, as the decision in *Bell v. Bell* implies.

193. As a result of the ills caused by section 7(3), section 7(9) was enacted in 1992: When a court grants a decree of divorce in respect of a marriage the patrimonial consequences of which are according to the rules of South African private international law governed by the law of a foreign state, the court shall have the same power as a competent court of a foreign state concerned would have had at that time to order that assets be transferred from one spouse to the other spouse. This provision renders the redistribution discretion of the *lex domicilii matrimonii* available regardless of how section 7(3) is interpreted. If section 7(9) applies, the typical limitations of section 7(3) of the Divorce Act would not apply. A redistribution may be effected on the ground of the contribution of one spouse to the other's estate, for purposes of the maintenance of spouse and children or the payment of a *solatium* to an innocent spouse if the *lex domicilii matrimonii* allows this.[479] The application of section 7(3) ought to enter the equation only when the foreign law lacks a satisfactory redistribution discretion.[480] The enactment of section 7(9) seems to be aimed at achieving a more accommodating stance in respect of foreign marriages, to, in effect, close the 'gap' occasioned by section 7(3) in cases where the proprietary consequences of a marriage are governed by a foreign legal system. Nonetheless, it is difficult to justify the insertion of this section into the Divorce Act. While underlying considerations of conflicts justice may have prompted this piece of legislative reform, its insertion has not solved our problems in this area of the law at all.[481] The social aim of providing fairness in property allocation upon divorce may yet again be frustrated should the foreign *lex causae* not provide for (satisfactory) redistribution of assets upon divorce. It may be asked whether, in such a situation, the judge would again find the pull of the *lex fori* strong enough to justify the application of South African law (provided, of course, that the requirements of section 7(3), such as the existence of an antenuptial contract, are met).

194. It is clear that South African PIL is not settled in regard to the classification of redistribution of assets upon divorce. Recently, the urgent need for reform in this area of the law was voiced yet again by Josman A.J., in *Esterhuizen v. Esterhuizen*:[482]

> The fact that the law in this respect is both complex and not entirely satisfactory is not, however, something that the Courts can set right by means of interpretation. The Legislature must decide whether it wishes the *lex domicilii matrimonii* principle to remain intact, even if it does produce anomalous results in some circumstances, or whether it wishes the benefits of Section 7(3) of the

478. Neels 2001 *TSAR* 692; Neels, 2001–2002, 9–10.
479. Neels 2003 *SALJ* 887.
480. Neels 1993–2000, 11.
481. See Roodt 1995 *THRHR* 194; 440; Roodt 2006 *THRHR* 546 for criticism of s. 7(9) and a call for reform.
482. 1999 (1) SA 492 (C): see discussion *supra*.

Divorce Act to apply to all marriages out of community of property, irrespective of whether this arises *ex lege* or by virtue of an antenuptial contract. The latter will be more even-handed in this application but this is a policy decision to be taken by the Legislature. It will entail the repeal of Section 7(9) of the Divorce Act.

VI. Personal Consequences

195. Personal consequences of marriage are those invariable consequences in regard to the personal relation of the parties to one another, which cannot be changed by way of an antenuptial contract.[483] According to Kahn personal consequences include the following:

> [T]he personal rights and duties of the spouses which owe from the marital relationship, for instance, the duty of conjugal fidelity and the right and duty of support; the effect of marriage on the legal capacity of the parties, such as the capacity to contract, to acquire and alienate property, to sue and be sued, to carry on a business; legal transactions between husband and wife, for example, the capacity of the spouses to contract with, make donations to,[484] and sue each other, and the power of the wife to bind her husband's credit for household necessaries; the effect of marriage on the wife's name'.[485]

196. There is substantial Roman-Dutch authority for the conflicts rule that the personal consequences of a marriage are governed by the *lex domicilii* of the spouses at the time that the act in question took place.[486] However, in terms of the Domicile Act[487] a wife may now acquire her own domicile, independent from that of her husband, and therefore it may be difficult to decide whose domicile is decisive if the parties were domiciled in different places at the time of the act or transaction.[488] In this regard the rule will have to be qualified, probably by referring to the party's domicile that has the most significant connection with the act or transaction.[489] When it comes to commercial contracts with third parties, a married

483. Edwards & Kahn *LAWSA: Conflict*, para. 308.
484. Section 22 of the Matrimonial Property Act 88 of 1984 has abolished the prohibition on donations between spouses during the subsistence of the marriage.
485. Hahlo & Kahn *Husband and Wife*, 622–623.
486. Bynkershoek *Observationes Tumultuariae*, IV 3083 3260; Rodenburg *Tractatus de Jure Conjugum*, 2 (paras alt.), 1 1, 107; Van der Keessel *Praelectiones Iuris*, 1 2 27; Voet *Commentarius*, 5 1 101. For case law on this topic, see *Kent v. Salmon* 1910 TPD 637; *Powell v. Powell* 1953 (4) SA 380 (W); *Perrott-Humphrey v. Perrott-Humphrey* 1967 (3) SA 304 (W) and see Edwards & Kahn *LAWSA: Conflict*, para. 308; Forsyth *Private International Law*, 292ff; Hahlo & Kahn *Husband and Wife*, 623ff as well as Van Rooyen *Kontrak*, 120ff for discussions of the rule and the cases.
487. 3 of 1992 s. 1(1).
488. The South African Law Commission did not consider this problem in their Report on Domicile 1990 (Project 60).
489. Kahn 1992 *ASSAL* 677.

woman should not be entitled to rely on contractual incapacity in terms of her domiciliary law (if such an incapacity exists) if she had contractual capacity according to the *lex loci contractus* or probably the putative proper law of the contract.[490] Therefore domicile should not be decisive in the case of commercial transactions with third parties when the contractual capacity of a spouse is in issue.

VII. Spousal Maintenance

197. This is an ancillary claim which arises in a divorce action and, as such, it is governed by the *lex fori* in terms of section 2(3) of the Divorce Act.[491] Kahn refers to maintenance after divorce as falling to be governed by the court's own law whether *qua lex fori* or *qua lex domicilii*.[492] A number of scholars agree,[493] and Josman J. adopted this view in *Esterhuizen v. Esterhuizen*.

198. In *Hassan v. Hassan*,[494] however, Hugo J. distinguished between the duty to maintain *stante matrimonio* and after the dissolution of a marriage. The judge did not wish to separate this aspect from other issues relating to the patrimonial effects of the dissolution because the maintenance that may be payable after dissolution of the marriage depends largely on the relative financial position of the parties after dissolution. The Family Law (Scotland) Act of 1985 was applied, and more particularly section 8 (orders for payment of capital sum, transfer of property, periodical allowance, incidental orders), section 9 (transitional provisions) and section 13 (order for periodical allowances).

VIII. Custody of Minors

199. As an issue arising during divorce proceedings, custody of minors is governed by the *lex fori*.[495] It is submitted that the best interests of the child will be decisive.[496]

490. Hahlo & Kahn *Husband and Wife*, 624. See also the distinction drawn *supra* in para. 79 between status and the incidents of status. While status should be ascertained with reference to the *lex domicilii* of the individual, this principle does not necessarily apply to the incidents of status: see Huber *De Conflictu Legum*, secs. 12 and 13. See also the discussion of contractual capacity of married women *supra* paras 80ff.
491. 70 of 1979. See *Holland v. Holland* 1973 (1) SA 897 (T), and *supra* para. 179.
492. Kahn 1979 *ASSAL* 496.
493. Heaton & Schoeman 2000 *THRHR* 145; Neels 1992 *TSAR* 337; Neels 2001 *TSAR* 696; Roodt 1995 *THRHR* 211.
494. 1998 (2) SA 598 (D).
495. Section 2(3) of the Divorce Act 70 of 1979. See also Kahn 1979 *ASSAL* 496, as well as *supra* para. 179.
496. See also Barrie 2009 *TSAR* 562.

IX. Child Support

200. In the absence of clear authority, Spiro submits that the parents' duty to support their children should be governed by the *lex domicilii* of the child.[497]

X. Legitimacy, Legitimization and Adoption

201. The modern trend is to eliminate the disqualifications attached to the status of illegitimacy. This distinction between legitimate and illegitimate children is losing force in South Africa too.[498] Should a South African court, in terms of its conflict rule, be referred to a foreign *lex causae* that does not distinguish between legitimate and illegitimate children, the child concerned should be regarded as legitimate in South Africa if the incidents attached to her status as a 'child' in the foreign legal system accord with those of a legitimate child at South African law.[499]

202. As far as choice of law is concerned, Innes C.J. drew a clear distinction between the issues of validity of marriage and the status of legitimacy in the Appellate Division decision in *Seedat's Executors v. The Master (Natal)*:[500] '... it is essential to bear in mind the distinction between the points to be decided in each instance. With regard to the wife, the issue is the validity of the marriage to which she was a party; with regard to the children the issue is their right to the status of legitimacy. The wife's position cannot be considered apart from the marriage, but the position of the children may be'.[501]

203. This prepared the way for the enunciation of an independent conflicts rule to determine the legitimacy of the children, namely the *lex domicilii originis*. The crucial moment for the determination of legitimacy is at birth and thus the issue was traditionally referred to the law of the domicile of origin.[502] However, at the time reference to the domicile of origin complicated matters. According to Roman-Dutch law the domicile of origin of a legitimate child (a child born in wedlock) was that of her father at the time of her birth, while an illegitimate child (a child born out of wedlock) followed her mother's domicile.[503] Therefore the inquiry into the child's domicile of origin focused on whether the child was legitimate or not, the

---

497. *Parent and Child*, 506.
498. The Children's Act 38 of 2005 no longer relies on this distinction. In terms of s. 9 of Ch. 2 of the Constitution of the Republic of South Africa 108 of 1996 there may not be unfair discrimination by the state or any other person against anyone on the grounds of, *inter alia*, birth. The Births and Deaths Registration Act 51 of 1992 provides for the registration of children born of customary unions and religious marriages as legitimate children.
499. Edwards & Kahn *LAWSA: Conflict*, para. 313; *Cheshire-North*, 1151; *Dicey-Morris, Vol. 2*, 1046–1047.
500. 1917 AD 302.
501. At 311–312.
502. *Seedat's Executors v. The Master (Natal)* 1917 AD 302 at 310, 314; *Hamid v. Minister of the Interior*, 1954 (4) SA 241 (T) at 247B–C; *Righetti v. Pinchin and Another* 1955 (3) SA 338 (D) at 342H–343A; *Von Wintzingerode v. Von Wintzingerode* 1964 (2) SA 618 (T) at 621C–D.
503. *Govu v. Stuart* (1903) 24 NLR 440; Kahn *Domicile*, 17.

very issue that had to be determined with reference to the domicile of origin.[504] In *Seedat* it was easy to refer the issue of legitimacy to the law of the domicile of origin, since both parents were, at the time of the birth of the children concerned, domiciled in India. Therefore there was no real need to determine which parents' domicile was decisive.

204. However, in a subsequent case, *Hamid v. Minister of the Interior*,[505] matters were complicated by the fact that the parents of the child had had different domiciles at the time of his birth. In such a case it was impossible to refer to the law of the domicile of origin[506] since the child's legitimacy (or illegitimacy) determined which parents' domicile was decisive. Hill A.J. decided that, in such a case, reference should be made to the domicile of the father at the time of the birth of the child: 'Legitimacy is a matter of status and has therefore to be determined by the law obtaining in the child's domicile of origin, i.e., by the law of his father's domicile at the time of his birth ...'[507]

205. This conflicts rule, namely that legitimacy should be determined by the law of the father's domicile at the time of the child's birth,[508] also finds support in English law.[509] Why the father's domicile should take precedence over that of the mother is an open question, but nevertheless an important one, since a baby is bound to have her first home with her mother.[510]

206. However, it seems as if the reform brought about by the Domicile Act[511] has solved the problems regarding the determination of the *domcilium originis*.[512] In terms of section 2 of this Act a child's domicile of origin is no longer linked to that of either of her parents, since a child does not have a domicile of dependence anymore. In other words, it is no longer necessary to establish whether a child is

504. Welsh 1947 *LQR* 65 at 70.
505. 1954 (4) SA 241 (T).
506. As it was understood at common law, before the inurement of s. 2 of the Domicile Act 3 of 1992: see *supra*.
507. At 247B. Although the equation of the child's domicile of origin to the domicile of his father at the time of his birth was, at the time, certainly not correct, since the issue of legitimacy had not yet been determined, the gist of the decision seems to have been that the father's domicile at birth should be decisive.
508. See Kahn 1955 *SALJ* 24 at 25.
509. *Cheshire-North* (13th edn), 895 who indicates that it is the domicile of the *natural* father that is decisive. See also Guttman 1959 *ICLQ*, 678 at 686 who proposes the following rule for common law as well as civil law systems: 'Legitimacy is to be governed by the *lex domicilii*, or the personal law [that would indicate *nationality* as the connecting factor in civil-law systems], of the man who is alleged to be the mother's husband or alternatively of any other man who is proved to have lived with the mother in such circumstances that any child of hers is legitimate by his personal law at the time the child was conceived or was born'.
510. See *Cheshire-North* (13th edn), 895–896 who answers the question with reference to the emphasis placed by Continental systems on the relationship between father and child: see also Guttman 1969 *ICLQ* 678 at 687.
511. 3 of 1992.
512. There is no indication in the South African Law Commission's Working Paper on Domicile 20 (Project 60) that the conflict rule in regard to legitimacy was considered.

legitimate or not in order to assign a domicile to her at birth. In terms of section 2 of the Act a child's domicile is at the place with which she is most closely connected, and if she shares a home with one or both of her parents, that parental home is presumed to be her domicile.[513] Thus it has become quite simple to determine a child's domicile, even at birth, in terms of the new Act. Since it no longer hinges on the question of legitimacy, the domicile of a child at birth could again become the connecting factor for conflicts purposes. This would indeed be appropriate: since it is the child's status that is at stake, reference should be made to *her* domicile, and not to that of her father.[514]

207. Since legitimation affects the status of the child concerned, domicile should constitute the connecting factor for choice-of-law purposes. In view of the changes brought about by the Domicile Act[515] in regard to the determination of the domicile of a child[516] it is submitted that the issue of legitimation (in other words, whether the child could have been, and was, in fact, legitimated) should be referred to the domicile of the child either at birth or at the time of legitimation.

208. Regarding adoption, there is no direct authority in South African PIL, but it is submitted that, since adoption changes the status of the adopted child, it should be governed by the domicile of that child at the time of adoption.[517] The Children's Act[518] provides for inter-country adoption[519] among other things, and gives effect to the 1993 Hague Convention on Protection of Children and Co-operation in respect of Inter-country Adoption. Chapter 19 of this Act came into effect on 1 April 2010.

XI. Guardianship

209. A South African court which has jurisdiction to make an order regarding guardianship will apply its own law.[520] In the absence of a court order, issues relating to guardianship are governed by the *lex domicilii*.[521] It is not clear from *Ex Parte Van Dam* whose domicile is decisive, since this case was decided before the abolition of the child's domicile of dependence. However, it is submitted that it should

---

513. In terms of s. 2(1) a child is domiciled at the place with which he is most closely connected, while s. 2(2) contains the presumption that, should a child have his home with one or both of his parents, that parental home will be his domicile.
514. See further Schoeman 1999 *SALJ* 288.
515. 3 of 1992.
516. See s. 2 of the Act discussed *supra*.
517. Spiro *Parent and Child*, 499.
518. 38 of 2005.
519. See *De Gree and Another v. Webb and Others (Centre for Child Law as Amicus* Curiae) 2007 (5) SA 184 (SCA) and Central *Authority v. H* 2008 (1) SA 49 (SCA) with regard to inter-country adoption under the Children's Act.
520. Forsyth *Private International Law*, 311.
521. *Ex Parte Van Dam*, 1973 (2) SA 182 (W) at 182H–183A. See also Edwards & Kahn *LAWSA: Conflict*, para. 316.

be the child's domicile at the relevant time. The best interests of the child[522] will play an important role. The *lex situs* may be relevant should the issue concern immovable property.[523]

XII. Pre- and Postnuptial Contracts

210. In South African domestic law, unlike the position in many other countries, the default matrimonial property regime is one of community of property. Therefore, if parties wish to marry out of community of property they have to conclude an antenuptial contract. This contract must be registered in a deeds registry within three months of its execution or within such an extended period as the court may allow on application.[524]

211. Regarding the formal validity of 'foreign' antenuptial contracts, section 87(2) of the Deeds Registries Act[525] determines that, if an antenuptial contract is executed outside South Africa it must be attested by a notary or otherwise entered into in accordance with the law of the place of its execution (*lex loci contractus*), and it must be registered in a South African deeds registry within six months after the date of its execution or within such extended period as the court may on application allow. Section 86 of the same Act requires such registration in order for the contract to be valid against third parties.[526] Therefore, it would seem as if all antenuptial contracts executed outside South Africa must be registered in this manner. However, this would be extremely unfair towards parties who were living in another country when they were married and only later moved to South Africa. Thus the better view seems to be that section 87(2) only applies to antenuptial contracts concluded between parties where the husband was, at the time of the execution of the antenuptial contract, domiciled in South Africa.[527]

212. In terms of our common law, an antenuptial contract entered into outside South Africa will be formally valid *inter partes* if it conforms to the *lex loci actus* or to the proper law of the contract.[528]

213. According to Kahn the essential validity of an antenuptial contract is governed by the *lex domicilii matrimonii* (the law of the husband's domicile at the time

522. *Ibid.*, 185D.
523. Spiro *Parent and Child*, 501–502.
524. Section 87(1) of the Deeds Registries Act 47 of 1937.
525. 47 of 1937.
526. See also *Ex Parte Spinazze and Another NNO*, 1985 (3) SA 650 (A) at 658A.
527. See *Ex Parte Van Borselen et Uxor*, 1942 TPD 206; *Ex Parte Taylor et Uxor*, 1949 (2) SA 254 (C). *Contra*, however, *Aspeling NO v. Alexander*, 1919 AD 139. See also Edwards & Kahn *LAWSA: Conflict*, para. 310; Forsyth *Private International Law*, 305–306; Hahlo & Kahn *Husband and Wife*, 633; Roodt 2006 *THRHR* 220.
528. *Ex Parte Spinazze and Another NNO*, 1985 (3) SA 650 (A). See further Edwards 1986 *THRHR* 144; Spiro 1986 *THRHR* 139 as well as *supra* paras 105ff.

of marriage) as far as movables are concerned and the *lex situs* as far as immovables are concerned.[529] However, one must agree with Forsyth that it would indeed be strange to adhere to the unitary principle (where movables and immovables are regarded as one unit) in the case where there is no antenuptial contract and then to disregard this principle where there is an antenuptial contract. He submits that the essential validity of an antenuptial contract should be governed by the *lex domicilii matrimonii* as far as movables and immovables are concerned.[530] This seems to be the better view.

214. The construction (or interpretation) and effect (rights and duties of the parties) of an antenuptial contract (for movables as well as immovables) are also governed by the *lex domicilii matrimonii*, unless there is an indication that the parties intended another legal system (by express or implied choice) to govern the interpretation and effect of their contract.[531]

215. The domicile of the husband features as a connecting factor in conflicts rules pertaining to patrimonial consequences of marriage, validity of the antenuptial contract (whether formal or substantive), construction and legal effect of the antenuptial contract. Roodt has investigated the scope that exists for party choice, and recommends that it be considered a factor in the conflicts rules that apply in the context of antenuptial contracts.[532] She suggests that the principle and limitations of party autonomy be allowed to influence future law reform of common law conflict rules that are open to constitutional challenge.

216. As far as capacity to enter into an antenuptial contract is concerned, the *lex domicilii* (of the particular party at the time of the execution of the antenuptial contract) will probably govern movables, while the *lex situs* will apply to immovable property. There is, however, no clear authority on this point.[533]

217. A postnuptial contract will be recognized in South Africa, provided that the *lex domicilii* of the spouses at the time of the execution of the postnuptial contract allows for such postnuptial contracts. This applies to movable, as well as immovable property.[534] It is not clear whose domicile will be decisive should the spouses have different domiciles.

XIII. Artificial Insemination, Surrogacy

218. Chapter 19 of the Children's Act contains provisions on surrogacy.[535] Section 292(1)(b)-(e) of the Children's Act sets out the requirements for validity of

529. *Husband and Wife*, 635.
530. *Private International Law*, 303.
531. Hahlo & Kahn *Husband and Wife*, 635; Forsyth *Private International Law*, 304.
532. Roodt *THRHR* 215; 367; 546.
533. Forsyth *Private International Law*, 304; Hahlo & Kahn *Husband and Wife*, 633–634.
534. Hahlo & Kahn *Husband and Wife*, 636–637.
535. Sections 292–303 of Act 38 of 2005.

a surrogate motherhood agreement in terms of South African law. The validity of a surrogate motherhood agreement is governed by South African law if the agreement was concluded in South Africa and at least one commissioning parent as well as the surrogate mother and her husband or partner are domiciled in South Africa at the time of entering into the agreement. The meaning and interpretation of domicile as a connecting factor in South African law is governed by the Domicile Act.[536] The definition of 'parents' in the Act is yet to be amended to include the commissioning parents of a surrogate child.[537] Couples who do not have their domicile in South Africa are excluded from commissioning a surrogate child. At least one of the commissioning parents must be domiciled in South Africa to qualify for the legal protection offered by the Act.

The requirement concerning the domicile of the surrogate mother and her partner may be disposed of on good cause shown. The confirmation by the High Court within whose area of jurisdiction the commissioning parent or parents are domiciled or habitually resident is required under subsection (e). This provision indicates when South African law applies to a surrogate motherhood agreement, instead of identifying a single connecting factor for the category of validity of a surrogate motherhood agreement that would point in the direction of the applicable law.[538] The rule safeguards the opportunity for the South African judiciary to exercise discretion and control over surrogacy agreements, and ensures that the public interests of the forum can be safeguarded. The unilateral structure of the rule also precludes the insertion of any choice of law or choice of court clauses into the agreement. As such, the parties do not have the freedom to select the law applicable to their agreement, and the rule itself finds application by virtue of designating the court that is competent to confirm the surrogate motherhood agreement. If a South African court has jurisdiction to confirm, it will apply the *lex fori*.

536. 3 of 1992.

537. Section 2(3) of the Domicile Act 3 of 1992.

538. A formula that identifies which law applies if the surrogate motherhood agreement is concluded in South Africa, and which law applies if it is concluded in another state, would be readily identifiable as a multilateral conflicts rule.

Chapter 7. Succession Law

§1. *Lex Successionis*

219. In terms of South African PIL the scission principle applies in so far as a distinction is made between movable and immovable property. Immovable property is generally governed by the *lex situs*, while the *lex domicilii* dominates in respect of movable property. Regarding movable property, the unitary principle is adhered to: all movables, wherever situated, are governed by the same legal system, usually the *lex domicilii* of the decedent or testator at the time of death.[539]

§2. Intestate Succession

220. Intestate succession occurs where the deceased did not leave a will or where a will or certain sections of a will are invalid. The *lex situs* determines all issues regarding immovable property, while the *lex ultimi domicilii* (the law of the last domicile) of the decedent governs movable property.[540]

§3. Testamentary Disposition

I. Validity of Wills

221. The capacity to make a will disposing of movable property is governed by the *lex domicilii* of the testator at the time of making the will. In respect of immovable property capacity to make a will is subjected to the *lex situs*.[541]

222. In regard to capacity to take under a will, the *lex situs* governs immovable property,[542] but the position regarding movable property is uncertain. Forsyth proposes that the *lex domicilii* of the beneficiary at the time of execution of the will should govern the issue.[543]

223. The intrinsic (essential) validity of a will concerns issues such as whether a wife or children should receive a *ius relictae* or a *legitimo portio*; whether witnesses to a will may benefit under it; rules which restrict the freedom of testation; etc.[544] Essential validity of a will is governed by the *lex situs* as far as immovable property is concerned and the *lex ultimi domicilii* of the testator as far as movable property is concerned.[545]

539. Edwards & Kahn *LAWSA: Conflict*, para. 318; Corbett, Hofmeyr, Kahn *Succession*, 612.
540. Edwards & Kahn *LAWSA: Conflict*, para. 319; Corbett, Hofmeyr, Kahn *Succession*, 614–615.
541. Edwards & Kahn *LAWSA: Conflict*, para. 320; Corbett, Hofmeyr, Kahn *Succession*, 616–617ff.
542. Edwards & Kahn *LAWSA: Conflict*, para. 320; Corbett, Hofmeyr, Kahn *Succession*, 618.
543. *Private Intenational Law*, 376–377.
544. See Forsyth *Private International Law*, 401.
545. Corbett, Hofmeyr, Kahn *Succession*, 631–632.

224. The formal validity of wills in South African PIL is now almost exclusively governed by section 3*bis* of the Wills Act.[546] Section 3*bis* applies to any will, irrespective of when it was executed, with the exclusion of a will made by a South African citizen otherwise than in writing[547] and a will made by a person who died before 4 December 1970.[548]

225. Section 3*bis* (1)(a) provides that the formal validity of a will as far as movable and immovable property are concerned, is governed by the internal law (thus excluding *renvoi*) of either of the following *leges causae*:

- the *lex loci actus*;
- the *lex domicilii* of the testator at the time of making the will or at the time of death;
- the law of the habitual residence of the testator at the time of making the will or at the time of death; or
- the law of the state or territory of which the testator was a citizen at the time of making the will or at the time of death.

226. Section 3*bis* (1)(b) provides an additional *lex causae* for immovable property, namely the *lex situs*.

227. Apart from the above available *leges causae* for testing the formal validity of a will, the following additional *leges causae* are provided for in specific instances:

- Section 3*bis* (1)(c) provides that a will in which a power conferred by any instrument is exercised or a duty imposed by any instrument is performed, will be formally valid if it complies with the internal law of the state or territory in which the instrument was executed.
- Section 3*bis* (1)(d) provides that a will which revokes another will or a portion of a will which is formally valid in terms of section 3*bis* (1)(a), (b) or (c) will be formally valid if it complies with the internal law of the relevant section 3*bis* (1)(a), (b) or (c) in terms of which the revoked will or portion is valid.[549]
- Section 3*bis* (1)(e) provides that a will which was executed on board a vessel or aircraft will be formally valid if it complies with the internal law of the state or territory in which such vessel or aircraft was registered at the time of execution, or with which it was otherwise most closely connected at the time.

546. 7 of 1953. Section 3*bis* of this Act was modeled on the Draft Convention on the Formal Validity of Wills which emanated from the Ninth Session of the Hague Conference on Private International Law (1960): see Corbett, Hofmeyr, Kahn *Succession*, 621 and Forsyth *Private International Law* 398 n. 216.

547. Section 3*bis* (4)(a).

548. Section 3*bis* (4)(b).

549. See Neels 2007 *ICLQ* 613 for a detailed analysis of s. 3*bis* (1)(d).

228. Section 3*bis* also addresses a few other issues. In terms of section 3*bis* (2) any requirement of the internal law of any other state or territory in terms of which a testator of a particular age or nationality or having any other personal qualification is to observe special formalities in the execution of a will, or a witness to a will is to possess certain qualifications, shall be construed as a requirement relating to form only. Section 3*bis* (3) provides that if there are in force in any state or territory two or more systems of internal law relating to the form of wills, the internal law to be applied for the purposes of this section shall be the internal law determined in accordance with any relevant rule in force in the state or territory in question or, if there is no such rule in force therein, the internal law with which the testator was most closely connected at the time of his death, if the matter is to be determined with reference to the circumstances prevailing at his death, or at the time of the execution of the will in any other case.

229. Section 3*bis* has not replaced the common law regarding the formal validity of wills. However, application of the common law is essentially restricted to the case of a person who has died before the commencement of this section, namely 4 December 1970, or to a will by a South African citizen that is not in writing.[550] In terms of the common law the formal validity of a will in respect of immovable property is governed by either the *lex situs* or the *lex loci actus*.[551] In regard to movable property the *lex loci actus* or the *lex domicilii* of the testator (probably either at the time of the execution of the will or at the time of death) will determine formal validity.[552]

II. Revocation of Wills

230. The formal validity of a revoking will has already been dealt with.[553] Regarding other issues related to the revocation of a will, it is submitted that the *lex situs* will apply to immovable property and the *lex domicilii*, probably the *lex domicilii* of the testator at the time of revocation, in respect of movable property.[554]

231. However, there is an exception to the above which relates to both movable and immovable property, namely where a legal system provides for the revocation of previous wills upon marriage. Since this aspect is usually classified as belonging to the category of proprietary consequences of marriage and, as such, determined in accordance with the *lex domicilii matrimonii*, it is submitted that revocation will also be governed by the *lex domicilii matrimonii*.[555]

550. Section 3*bis* (4)(a) and (b).
551. Corbett, Hofmeyr, Kahn *Succession*, 620.
552. *Ibid.*, 619.
553. In terms of s. 3*bis* (1)(d): see *supra* para. 234.
554. Compare Corbett, Hofmeyr, Kahn *Succession*, 632ff.
555. Compare Corbett, Hofmeyr, Kahn *Succession*, 594.

III. Interpretation of Wills

232. Whether a will disposes of movable or immovable property, interpretation is governed by the *lex domicilii* of the testator at the time of execution of the will. However, in respect of immovable property, the *lex situs* may apply in regard to immovable property should the *lex domicilii* produce a result which is illegal or impossible to give effect to by the *lex situs*.[556]

556. Edwards & Kahn *LAWSA: Conflict*, para. 320.

Part III. Annex: International Civil Procedure (ICP)

Chapter 1. Sources of ICP (National Law, International Conventions)

233. In South African PIL the rules of international civil procedure are mainly found in common law (which includes court decisions) and national statute law (which includes accession to international conventions).

Chapter 2. The Principle of *Lex Fori*

234. When a South African court assumes jurisdiction in a PIL matter the *lex fori* (South African law) governs all matters relating to procedure. Contrary to the trend in many other common-law jurisdictions, procedure is interpreted widely to include all procedures pertaining to the commencement and institution of civil proceedings in court (e.g., rules relating to pleadings, etc.); all court procedures; questions relating to evidence in court (e.g., admissibility of evidence, competency of witnesses, etc.); the execution of judgments and the taxation of costs.[557] Whether a matter pertains to substance or procedure is a matter of classification.[558] The courts revert to the *via media* approach to classification,[559] but it is submitted that, in the context of the substance/procedure dichotomy, such an approach is unnecessary and has been applied too restrictively.

235. In regard to the law of evidence a distinction is often drawn between the *facta probanda* (facts relevant to the issue) which are regarded as substantive and, as such, governed by the *lex causae* and the *facta probantia* (the manner of proof) which are regarded as procedural and, as such, governed by the *lex fori*.[560] However, the onus of proof is classified as substantive and therefore it is governed by the *lex causae*.[561] Presumptions are generally regarded as procedural, except where a presumption of death affects the vesting of assets or private-law status.[562]

236. Regarding damages (in contract and delict), the *lex causae* determines the kinds of damages which may be recovered as well as the quantum of damages.[563] However, the form of remedy, for example, whether it involves the payment of money or compulsory performance, is determined by the *lex fori*.[564]

557. Edwards & Kahn *LAWSA: Conflict*, para. 343; Forsyth *Private International Law*, 24.
558. See *supra* paras 58ff.
559. See e.g., *Laurens v. Von Höhne* 1993 (2) SA 104 (W); *Society of Lloyd's v. Price*; *Society of Lloyd's v. Lee* 2005 3 SA 549 (T); *Society of Lloyd's v. Romahn* 2006 4 SA 23 (K); *Society of Lloyd's v. Price*; *Society of Lloyd's v. Lee* 2006 5 SA 393 (HHA).
560. Edwards & Kahn *LAWSA: Conflict*, para. 343. See also *Laurens v. Von Höhne* 1993 (2) SA 104 (W) at 117I–J.
561. *Laurens v. Von Höhne* 1993 (2) SA 104 (W) at 112I–J.
562. Edwards & Kahn *LAWSA: Conflict*, para. 343.
563. *Ibid.*; Forsyth *Private International Law*, 24–25; Van Rooyen *Kontrak*, 200ff.
564. Edwards & Kahn *LAWSA: Conflict*, para. 343; Spiro *General Principles*, 76.

Chapter 3. National Jurisdiction

237. In order to provide a clear picture of the basis of national jurisdiction, it is important to understand the principles that support the assumption of jurisdiction. It is also important to distinguish PIL jurisdiction to the extent that the emphasis in this regard may differ from that in purely domestic cases. An attempt will be made in this chapter to provide a general overview of the principles upon which national jurisdiction is based, with particular reference to PIL matters.

238. National (or domestic) jurisdiction is the right or authority, under South African law, of a court to entertain actions or other legal proceedings,[565] a right or authority which is granted to the court by the state. Historically, a state could only bind persons and property within its territorial boundaries,[566] and thus jurisdiction was based on territorial sovereignty.[567] This gave rise to the rule *actor sequitur forum rei*, which meant that a defendant should be sued in the forum of the place where she is domiciled, since that court has effective control over the defendant.[568] In similar vein it was argued that proceedings relating to immovable property should be instituted in the *forum rei sitae*, since the court of the area where the property is situated, has effective control over such property.[569]

239. The doctrine of effectiveness thus became the basis for the assumption of jurisdiction and, even though the contemporary meaning of effectiveness is far removed from the original meaning of 'territorial control', the principle is, to this day, acknowledged as a realistic foundation for the assumption of jurisdiction. In modern law 'effectiveness' pertains rather to the ability of the court to give a meaningful judgment, in the sense that the court has *sufficient* control, and not necessarily *territorial* (or *physical*) control, over the property or the defendant to render its judgment potentially[570] effective.

240. In order to give effect to this doctrine of effectiveness, Pollak has argued that actions should be classified with reference to the nature of the relief sought. This is contrary to the Roman-law classification,[571] which was adopted by Roman-Dutch law,[572] into *actiones in personam*, *actiones in rem* and *actiones mixta* (a category which was added in the Middle Ages). In terms of this classification of actions

565. Pollak *Jurisdiction*, 1. See also Voet *Commentarius*, 2 1 1.
566. Compare the well-known Roman maxim enunciated in D 2 1 20: *extra territorium ius dicenti impune non paretur* (one who administers justice beyond the limits of his territory may be disobeyed with impunity).
567. D 2 1 20. Compare also J. Bristowe, quoted by Pollak *Jurisdiction*, 17, in *Schlimmer v. Executrix in Estate of Rising*, 1904 TH 108 at 111: 'The jurisdiction of the courts of every country is territorial in its extent and character, for it is derived from the sovereign power, which is necessarily limited by the boundaries of the State over which it holds sway'.
568. C 3 13 2; C 3 19 3.
569. C 3 19 3.
570. Assumption of jurisdiction does not carry a guarantee of effectiveness; yet there must be a reasonable belief that the judgment will be effective: Forsyth *Private International Law*, 170–171.
571. D 44 7 25*pr*.
572. Voet *Commentarius*, 44 7 9.

which focuses on the nature of the action, it was considered that the *forum rei domicilii* had jurisdiction in *actiones in personam*, the *forum rei sitae* in *actiones in rem* and either forum in the case of an *actio mixta*. However, Pollak indicates that, in an action concerning a *res*, a party may base her claim on either ownership of that *res*, which will mean that it is an *actio in rem*, or on contract, which will mean that it is an *actio in personam*. Thus different rules of jurisdiction will apply, depending on the nature of the claim.[573] Therefore Pollak argues that the nature of the relief sought, rather than the nature of the action, provides a proper basis for the assumption of jurisdiction, because '... a court may give an effective judgment in regard to one type of relief and not in regard to another type ... Since the principle of effectiveness underlies the views in regard to jurisdiction entertained by South African courts, it seems that the jurisdiction of the South African courts should depend not on the classification of actions which has come down to us from the Roman law but on the nature of the relief claimed'.[574]

241. The theory of jurisdiction is based on the nature of proceedings and the nature of relief sought.[575] While effectiveness should be regarded as the guiding norm, effectiveness is not the sole criterion for assuming jurisdiction, however. Other criteria include convenience, common sense, the interest of the court, social needs and justice.[576] A classification in terms of the relief sought would better satisfy the criterion of effectiveness than a classification according to the nature of the action. This does not mean that the nature of the relief sought is the only way of determining the proper jurisdictional connecting factor; submission to the jurisdiction of a court,[577] as well as other connecting factors, may very well meet the requirement of effectiveness. Therefore jurisdictional connecting factors should be selected with the principle of effectiveness in mind.

242. When it comes to the assumption of domestic jurisdiction in a conflicts case, the principle of effectiveness gains significance. Although the forum is primarily concerned with its domestic rules of jurisdiction, the possibility of its judgment being subjected to recognition and enforcement proceedings in a foreign country should be kept in mind.[578] If the court's assumption of jurisdiction meets the requirement of effectiveness, the potential for foreign recognition of its judgment

573. Pollak *Jurisdiction*, 14ff. See also Cook *Logical and Legal Bases*, 53ff; Pryles 1972 *ICLQ* 61–66.
574. Compare *Steytler NO v. Fitzgerald* 1911 AD 295 346; *Estate Agents Board v. Lek* 1979 (3) SA 1048 (A) at 1063F–G where both the nature of the proceedings and the nature of the relief claimed were named as possible bases of jurisdiction, either in the alternative or together, as well as *Hugo v. Wessels* 1987 (3) SA 837 (A) at 849H–J where specific mention was made of the doctrine of effectiveness.
575. Corbett, Hofmeyr, Kahn *Succession* 588.
576. Corbett, Hofmeyr, Kahn *Succession* 587.
577. See Pollak *Jurisdiction*, 19, as well as Beck 1983 *SALJ* 43 at 45.
578. Compare Beck 1983 *SALJ* 43 at 44–45: 'It is submitted that effectiveness is material in every matter ... for if the court were to give judgment without having jurisdiction over a material party to the action, the judgment could be reversed on appeal and would hardly be likely to find acceptance in other countries. This cannot be a general basis for effective judgments'.

will definitely be greater and this will contribute to international harmony. However, this is an area where statutory extension of jurisdiction, especially in the case of in personam jurisdiction, may create problems.

243. In a purely domestic matter, the plaintiff and defendant are domiciled or resident in the same country and it is even possible that they both reside or are domiciled within the same court's area of jurisdiction.[579] However, in a conflicts case the plaintiff and defendant are rarely situated within the same jurisdictional area and the basic premise that the plaintiff should sue the defendant in the forum where she resides or is domiciled (which also underlies the doctrine of effectiveness), has been questioned. Recognition of the public law dimension of choice of law is not widespread yet. To consider this dimension in conflict of laws is often associated with American experimentation during the policy revolution, and rejected for this reason.[580] The interest of the state in the assumption of jurisdiction by its courts is clear, however:

> The State may be interested in creating a forum for its own litigants. It may be interested in creating a local forum so that its laws can be properly applied. It may be interested in controlling the actions of its nationals [or, in common-law countries, its domiciliaries]. It may be interested in creating a forum that is convenient for resident witnesses. It may have an interest in creating a local forum for the adjudication of disputes that have an impact on the economic and social life of the State.[581]

244. Apart from the state's interests, the plaintiff and the defendant may also have very specific interests. Very often the financial burden will be greater for the plaintiff suing in the forum of the defendant than suing at home. Furthermore, the plaintiff will be more comfortable suing at home, since she is familiar with her forum's rules of procedure.[582] However, the plaintiff's interests are often overlooked or given less weight, since she is the one who institutes action and is regarded as disturbing the peace.[583] The defendant's interest of being sued in her home forum in familiar surroundings has always been protected by the maxim *actor sequitur forum rei*. Very often, though, it is the defendant who has refused to perform or has breached her obligations and therefore the blame for the resultant legal action rests squarely on her shoulders.[584]

245. Thus the balancing of the respective interests of the state, the plaintiff and the defendant may indeed be extremely complicated. It is submitted though, that the

---

579. For example, in South Africa where every division of the High Court has its own area of jurisdiction.
580. The emphasis placed by Currie and some of the other American commentators on the state's interest in choice-of-law matters has been severely criticized. See Nygh *Conflict*, 38; *contra* Roodt 2007 *CILSA* 77ff.
581. Smit 1972 *ICLQ* 335 at 351–352.
582. Von Mehren & Trautman 1966 *Harv. LR* 1121.
583. Smit 1972 *ICLQ* 335 at 351.
584. *Ibid.*, 350ff.

balancing of these interests should be done with the principle of effectiveness in mind. The creation of additional fora for private-international-law disputes, in the context of extension of jurisdiction, should not detract from the ability of a court to render a meaningful judgment. While it is true that there may be more than one forum that can justifiably assume jurisdiction in a dispute, it is important that the jurisdictional connecting factor secures a sufficiently close link between the parties and/or the property in dispute and the forum to enable the forum to render a meaningful judgment. A South African court will, for example, not hear a dispute between a peregrine plaintiff and a peregrine defendant[585] regarding a delict that was committed abroad; there must be a link that connects the action to the forum.

246. These jurisdictional links or connecting factors (e.g., domicile, residence, situation of property, place where delict was committed, etc.) provide the reason or justification for the court to assume jurisdiction. The selection of these *rationes jurisdictionis* should be based on the principle of effectiveness, which means that, while a jurisdictional connecting factor must be selected with the interests of the state, the plaintiff and the defendant in mind, effectiveness should be the guiding norm.

585. A peregrine is someone who is neither resident nor domiciled within the court's territory, whereas an *incola* is someone who is either resident or domiciled in the court's territory: see Forsyth *Private International Law*, 213.

Chapter 4. International Jurisdiction

247. There are specific grounds of international competence for particular categories of foreign judgments. These will be dealt with under the appropriate headings *infra*.

Chapter 5. Acceptability (Recognition) and Enforcement of Foreign Judgments

248. Recognition of a foreign judgment means that 'the domestic court acknowledges that it [the foreign judgment] has, within its own jurisdiction, the legal effect which the foreign court intended it to have'.[586] Enforcement of a foreign judgment means that 'the domestic court will compel the judgment debtor to comply with it [the foreign judgment]'.[587] In certain types of judgment, for example claims sounding in money, recognition and enforcement, go hand in hand: a South African forum will not order enforcement of a foreign judgment which it does not recognize. In these instances recognition is a *sine qua non* to the enforcement of a foreign judgment. However, in regard to status-related foreign judgments, such as divorce decrees, it is the recognition of a change in the private-law status of the individual(s) concerned that is at stake, and therefore enforcement as such does not occur.[588] Recognition of such a changed status, for example, a foreign divorce decree, may be crucial to the validity of a subsequent marriage.

249. The general requirements for the recognition and enforcement (where such is sought) of foreign judgments in South African law are as follows:[589] the foreign court must have had jurisdiction according to the South African rules of international jurisdiction; in other words, the foreign court must have had 'international competence' and the foreign judgment must be final.[590] In addition to these requirements a defendant may raise certain defenses against the recognition and enforcement of a foreign judgment; for example, that the judgment is against the public policy of the forum, or that it was obtained fraudulently, or that the enforcement of foreign penal or revenue laws is being sought, or that the judgment is not consistent with the forum's notions of natural justice.[591]

250. In regard to the enforcement of certain foreign judgments permission must be obtained in terms of the Protection of Businesses Act.[592] In terms of this Act the permission of the Minister of Economic Affairs (now Trade and Industry) is required for the enforcement in South Africa of any judgment, order, direction, arbitration award, interrogatory, *commission rogatoire*, letters of request or any other

586. Silberberg *Foreign Judgments*, 6.
587. *Ibid.*
588. Silberberg *Foreign Judgments*, 21.
589. See, in general, Edwards & Kahn *LAWSA: Conflict*, para. 345; Forsyth *Private International Law*, 419–420.
590. The fact that the foreign judgment is subject to appeal or that an appeal is pending, does not affect the finality of the judgment. However, a South African court has the discretion to stay proceedings until the foreign appeal has been finalized: see *Jones v. Krok* 1995 (1) SA 677 (A). Mere physical presence of the defendant suffices to confer international jurisdiction on a foreign court; see *Richman v. Ben-Tovim* 2007 (2) SA 283 at 289B and Schulze 2008 *SA Merc LJ* 61.
591. See Edwards & Kahn *LAWSA: Conflict*, para. 477.
592. 99 of 1978: for a discussion of this Act, see Edwards & Kahn *LAWSA: Conflict*, para. 346; Forsyth *Private International Law*, 466ff.

request delivered, given or issued or emanating from outside South Africa in connection with any civil proceedings and arising from any act or transaction[593] which occurred before or after the commencement of the Act and which pertains to mining, production, importation, exportation, refinement, possession, use or sale of or ownership to any material, of whatever nature, whether within, outside, into or from South Africa.[594] The Act further prohibits the recognition or enforcement of a judgment of a foreign court arising from any act or transaction (referred to in section 1(3) *supra*) which directs the payment of multiple or punitive damages,[595] irrespective of whether the Minister of Economic Affairs (now Trade and Industry) has granted his permission in terms of section 1(a) *supra*,[596] as well as, under certain circumstances and upon certain conditions, for the recovery of certain amounts paid by way of multiple or punitive damages.[597] The Act also prohibits the recognition or enforcement of any judgment, order, direction, arbitration award, interrogatory, *commission rogatoire*, letters of request or any other request delivered, in connection with any liability which arises from any bodily injury of any person resulting directly or indirectly from the consumption or use of or exposure to any natural resource of South Africa, whether unprocessed or partially or wholly processed, or any product containing or processed from any such material resource, given or issued outside South Africa or emanating from outside South Africa and which arises from any act or transaction referred to in section 1(3) *supra*, irrespective of whether the Minister of Economic Affairs (now Trade and Industry) has given his permission or not, unless the same liability would have arisen under South African law at the time of the occurrence of the event which gave rise to the liability.[598]

251. The provisions of the above Act (which may be regarded as statutory expressions of public policy) were apparently enacted to counter the tendency of American courts to interpret their federal anti-trust legislation in such a manner that the sovereignty of other states is infringed.[599] This Act has been widely criticized by writers on South African PIL and they have recommended a restrictive interpretation of its provisions.[600] The restrictive interpretation of the Act has also been confirmed by the Supreme Court of Appeal in *Richman v. Ben- Tovim*.[601] Furthermore, the South African Law Reform Commission is likely to make a finding on whether this Act poses unjustifiable obstacles to international cooperation when it finalizes

593. Section 1(a). There is a proposed amendment to the Act in terms of which 'arbitration awards' is to be deleted: see Van Niekerk and Schulze *International Trade*, 275.
594. Section 1(3). For a discussion of other provisions of this Act see Edwards *LAWSA: Conflict*, para. 346; Forsyth *Private International Law*, 466.
595. Section 1A(2) defines 'multiple or punitive damages' as that part of the amount awarded as damages which exceeds the amount determined by the court as compensation for the damage or loss actually sustained by the person to whom the damages have been awarded.
596. Section 1A(2).
597. Section 1B.
598. Section 1D.
599. See Edwards & Kahn *LAWSA: Conflict*, para. 346.
600. Forsyth *Private International Law*, 466ff and authors referred to by him.
601. See para. 11 of the decision. It was found, *inter alia* that the Act was not applicable to a claim for money due for professional services.

its project on Consolidation of legislation pertaining to international cooperation in civil matters.[602]

§1. Money Judgments

252. In terms of South African common law international competence in judgments sounding in money, whether from contract, delict or otherwise, may be established by the residence or domicile of the defendant within the jurisdictional area of the foreign court at the time of the institution of the action; or by submission to the jurisdiction of or the institution of a counterclaim in the foreign court.[603] When agreement of the parties confers jurisdiction upon a forum that would not have jurisdiction otherwise, it is referred to as prorogation.

253. South African courts assume jurisdiction in the following instances:[604]

(a) Where the plaintiff is an *incola* and the defendant is a foreign *peregrinus*. The attachment[605] of his property is essential for jurisdiction to be assumed and for purposes of an effective judgment. A recognized jurisdictional ground by itself does not suffice.
(b) Where the plaintiff is an *incola* and the defendant is a local *peregrinus* (i.e., a *peregrinus* of the division of the court, but not of the country) a recognized *ration jurisdictioinis* is essential.
(c) Where the plaintiff is a *peregrinus* (foreign or local) and the defendant is a foreign *peregrinus*, both a recognized jurisdictional ground as well as an arrest or attachment to found jurisdiction are essential.
(d) Where the plaintiff is a *peregrinus* (foreign or local) and the defendant is a local *peregrinus*, a jurisdictional ground alone suffices.[606]
(e) Where the defendant is an *incola*, the general rule *actor sequitur forum rei* applies.

The continued detention of a defendant or his passport after it is clear that the court has jurisdiction and that the judgment will be internationally enforceable, is illegal.[2] Civil detention to enforce a claim is unconstitutional.[607] Moreover, section 12 of the Constitution, which embodies the right to freedom and security of the person, has

602. Issue Paper 21 Project 121: Consolidation of legislation pertaining to international cooperation in civil matters 15–16. See Roodt 2004 (2) *Codicillus* 64; Roodt 2005 *CILSA* 15.
603. Edwards & Kahn *LAWSA: Conflict*, para. 346; Forsyth *Private International Law*, 420-438; Corbett, Hofmeyr, Kahn *Succession* 587.
604. *Ewing McDonald & Co. Ltd. v. M & M Products Co. Ltd.* 1991 (1) SA 252 (A); Forsyth *Private International Law*, 223.
605. In *Schmidt v. Weaving* 2009(1) SA 170 (SCA) it was found that, in order for the attachment of a peregrine defendant's interest in a close corporation to be valid; actual notice should be given to the corporation. A discussion of this case may be found in Schulze 2009 *Annual Survey* 134.
606. Section 28(1) of the Supreme Court Act forbids the attachment of person or property of someone who is resident in the Republic.
607. *Alliance Corporation Ltd. v. Blogg* [1999] 3 All SA 262 (W).

neutralized the doctrine of arrest. In *Bid Industrial Holdings (Pty) Ltd v. Strang*[608] the arrest of *peregrini ad fundandam jurisdictionem* was found to be unconstitutional on grounds of extensively infringing the defendant's rights under section 12 of the Constitution.[609] As long as any alternative effective course of action is available, the test for having the right limited will not be passed.[610] Cases of arrest to found or confirm jurisdiction are rare.[611]

254. In order to be enforced in South Africa, the foreign judgment must be final and conclusive and must be for a definite sum of money. Judgments for the payment of a tax or fine or penalty are not enforceable.[612]

255. To facilitate the enforcement of foreign money judgments, the Enforcement of Foreign Civil Judgments Act (South Africa)[613] was enacted. Like many Commonwealth countries, South Africa recognizes money judgments on the basis of registration. The doctrine of reciprocity forms no part of South African law and as such, the Enforcement of Foreign Civil Judgments Act (South Africa) does not require reciprocity as a condition for recognition. This Act facilitates enforcement by providing for the registration of foreign judgments rendered in countries that are designated by the clerk of the relevant magistrate's court and then has the same effect as a civil judgment of that court.[614] The judgment debtor must receive notice and may apply to have it set aside on the basis of certain specified grounds. The Minister of Justice designates states by means of an administrative process regardless of whether enforcement will be reciprocal.[615] Namibia is the only country designated in terms of this Act.[616]

256. In terms of the Foreign Civil Judgments Act 32 of 1988 (South Africa) a judgment is any final judgment or order for the payment of money rendered by any court in any civil proceedings which is enforceable by execution in the country in which it was given or made, excluding any judgment or order for the payment of tax, or a fine, or a penalty, or the periodical payment of sums of money towards the

---

608. 2008 (3) SA 355 (SCA).
609. Paragraphs 42–43 of the decision. See Eiselen 2008 *TSAR* 794, Oppong 2008 *JPIL* 311 and Schulze 2008 *Annual* Survey 167 for detailed analyses of the decision.
610. Section 36 of the Constitution provides that rights may be limited by laws of general application to an extent which is 'reasonable and justifiable in an open and democratic society based on human dignity, equality and freedom, taking into account all relevant factors, including (a) the nature of the rights; (b) the importance of the purpose of the limitation; (c) the nature and extent of the limitation; (d) the relation between the limitation and its purpose; and (e) less restrictive means to achieve the purpose'. See *Matiso v. Commanding Officer Port Elizabeth Prison* 1995 4 SA 631 (CC).
611. In general Harms *Civil Procedure* A4. 13, 16–17.
612. Edwards & Kahn *LAWSA: Conflict*, para. 346.
613. 32 of 1988.
614. See secs 2, 3. Section 2 provides for the designation of foreign countries by the Minister of Justice for purposes of the Act, as well as the withdrawal of designations.
615. See Roodt 2005 *CILSA* 15 for a critical perspective on the relevant legislation and the South African Law Reform Commission's Issue Paper and Discussion Document on Consolidated Legislation pertaining to Co-operation in Civil Matters (Project 121).
616. Section 2(1). See R 2094 *GG* 12726 RG 4548 of 7 Sep. 1990.

maintenance of any person.[617] A judgment registered in terms of this Act has the same effect as a civil judgment of the court at which the judgment was registered.[618] The Act also provides for the setting aside of a registered judgment on certain grounds, for example, that the judgment debtor did not receive proper or reasonable notice of the proceedings against him, that the judgment was obtained by fraud, that enforcement of the judgment would be contrary to the public policy of South Africa, that the judgment has become prescribed under either the South African law or the law of the designated country, etc.[619] The Act does not prevent a South African court from recognizing any judgment (other than a judgment the registration of which has been set aside in terms of section 5 of this Act) rendered by a foreign court of competent jurisdiction in any civil matter as conclusive of any matter of law or of fact decided in such judgment if such judgment could, before the commencement of the Act, have been so recognized by a South African court.[620] The Act also provides for a stay of execution of judgment, on conditions that the court may deem fit, where an appeal is pending or may be instituted against the judgment.[621] Furthermore, the Act contains certain presumptions regarding the jurisdiction of the foreign court,[622] as well as a prohibition on the removal or disposal of the judgment debtor's assets if such removal would prejudice the execution of judgment.[623]

§2. Judgments Relating to Property

257. Judgments in regard to both movable and immovable property will probably be recognized and enforced if such property was situated within the area of jurisdiction of the foreign court at the time of the proceedings.[624]

§3. Divorces, Judicial Separations and Annulments of Marriage

258. In this regard the Hague Convention on the Recognition of Divorces and Legal Separations[625] has had an important impact on the formulation of criteria of international competence for the recognition of foreign divorces, legal separations and annulments of marriage. Even though South Africa has not acceded to the Convention, the latest criteria for the recognition of foreign divorces, judicial separations, as well as annulments of marriage, have clearly been formulated with a view

617. Section 1.
618. Section 4.
619. See s. 5(1) for a comprehensive list.
620. Section 9.
621. Section 6.
622. Section 7(4) and (5).
623. Section 8.
624. Edwards & Kahn *LAWSA: Conflict*, para. 347; Forsyth *Private International Law*, 455ff.
625. 1968.

to possible accession in the future.[626] At present the Divorce Act[627] provides for the recognition by a South African court of the validity of a divorce order or an order for annulment of a marriage or for judicial separation[628] granted in a court of a foreign country or territory if, on the date on which the order was granted, either party to the marriage was:

- domiciled in the country or territory concerned, whether according to South African law or according to the law of that country or territory;
- ordinarily resident in that country or territory; or
- a national of that country or territory.

259. A most interesting feature of section 13 is that the interpretation of domicile as a jurisdictional connecting factor for purposes of international competence is extended beyond the traditional *lex fori* interpretation that is usually given in a choice-of-law context.[629] In other words, with regard to *domicilium* as a criterion for international competence, a foreign order for divorce or annulment of marriage or judicial separation will be recognized by a South African court if either of the parties was domiciled in the country or territory concerned, whether according to South African law or according to the law of that country or territory. This was no doubt done in order to eliminate one of the root causes of limping marriages, namely the different interpretations given to *domicilium* in different jurisdictions.

§4. Maintenance Orders

260. Maintenance orders are generally variable and therefore do not comply with the requirement of finality in terms of the common law requirements for the enforcement of foreign judgments. In South Africa the Reciprocal Enforcement of Maintenance Orders Act[630] governs enforcement of foreign maintenance orders. This Act provides for the registration of foreign maintenance orders made in proclaimed countries[631] by a maintenance court in South Africa by way of transmission through diplomatic channels.[632] Upon registration, such a maintenance order becomes an order of the maintenance court where it was registered.[633] In terms of The Reciprocal Enforcement of Maintenance Orders, Act 80 of 1963, a considerable number of states have been designated.[634]

---

626. See the South African Law Commission's Report on Domicile 1990 (Project 60), para. 6.54.
627. 70 of 1979 s. 13.
628. Even though judicial separation is no longer possible in South African law (s. 14 of the Divorce Act 70 of 1979), a South African court will recognize such an order issued by a foreign court.
629. See Kahn-Freund *General Problems*, 242.
630. 80 of 1963.
631. Section 2 provides for the designation of countries, as well as the withdrawal of such designations, by the Minister of Justice, for purposes of the Act.
632. Section 3.
633. Section 6.
634. Section 7. A considerable number of countries have been proclaimed by the state president: various Australian territories including Queensland and New South Wales; Lesotho; Botswana; Cocos Islands; Cyprus; the United Kingdom; Fiji; Guernsey; Isle of Man; Kenya; Mauritius; New Zealand; Nigeria; Norfolk Island; Northern Island; Zambia; Malawi; various provinces in Canada

261. The Reciprocal Enforcement of Maintenance Orders Act[635] provides for the transmission of maintenance orders made in South Africa to proclaimed countries.[636] The Act also makes provision for a full enquiry by the maintenance officer of the court for purposes of confirmation in South Africa of provisional maintenance orders made in proclaimed countries.[637] Provision is also made for an inquiry in South Africa in order to make a provisional maintenance order against a person resident in a proclaimed country who may be legally liable to maintain a person in South Africa and for the transmission of such a provisional maintenance order (together with all relevant information relating to the inquiry) to the foreign (proclaimed) country for confirmation. If so confirmed, the maintenance order becomes an order of the court that made the provisional order.[638]

262. Provision is also specifically made for the enforcement of maintenance orders in Africa in terms of the Reciprocal Enforcement of Maintenance Orders (Countries in Africa) Act.[639] The range of maintenance orders is wider than that of the Reciprocal Enforcement of Maintenance Orders Act, as it covers also the enforcement of provisional orders and orders for the attachment of earnings. Under the Reciprocal Enforcement of Maintenance Orders (Countries in Africa) Act, there is a simplified and accelerated administrative process for registration of maintenance orders made in Africa that does not depend on the Minister nor implies transmission through diplomatic channels. However, only Namibia has been validly designated in terms of this Act, since none of the other designations serve any purpose in post-apartheid South Africa.[640] To add to the confusion, a number of African countries have been designated under the 1963 Act.[641]

§5. Custody Orders

263. Although domicile, submission to jurisdiction, residence or mere physical presence may found international competence in regard to custody orders, such orders may be denied enforcement in a South African court because they frequently lack finality. Apart from this, the High Court is the upper guardian of all minor children within its area of jurisdiction and therefore the best interests of the child are of

---

including Ontario and Alberta; Sarawak; Singapore; Zimbabwe; Namibia; Hong Kong and US states such as California and Florida. Whether these states reciprocate with South Africa to enforce its maintenance orders is another matter, which the statute does not specifically require. Proc. R345 of 1960; Proc. R175 of 1962; Proc. R274 of 1963; Proc. R160 of 1970; Proc. R1 of 1971; Proc. R175 of 1971. Roodt 2005 *CILSA* 28 n. 81.

635. 80 of 1963.
636. Section 7.
637. Section 4.
638. Section 8.
639. 6 of 1989.
640. The formerly independent homelands were designated under the Reciprocal Enforcement of Maintenance Orders (Countries in Africa) Act 6 of 1989 Act. The independence of Transkei, Bophutatswana, Venda and Ciskei was never recognized outside of South Africa. These territories have been reincorporated into South Africa.
641. Roodt 2005 *CILSA* 20.

paramount importance. This means that the court will consider the order of the foreign court, but after having considered all the facts placed before it, will make its own order.[642]

§6. ADOPTION ORDERS

264. In principle, the domicile of the adopted child should found international competence, since adoption involves a change in the status of the child concerned. It may also be argued that residence (ordinary residence) should found international competence. However, once again, as the upper guardian of all minor children within its area of jurisdiction, the High Court will regard the best interests of the child as paramount so that a foreign order based upon a competent ground of jurisdiction may be refused.[643]

§7. FOREIGN ARBITRAL AWARDS

265. South Africa is a party to the New York Convention on the Recognition and Enforcement of Foreign Arbitral Awards (1958), the provisions of which have been implemented by the Recognition and Enforcement of Foreign Arbitral Awards Act.[644] This Act provides that a foreign arbitral award may upon application to the High Court, be made an order of the court and enforced as such.[645] The court may refuse to grant the application on a number of grounds, including the following: enforcement of the award would be against the public policy of the forum; the principles of natural justice were not adhered to and the defendant did not receive proper notice of proceedings or was not given an opportunity to present his or her case or the award was not a final one.[646] South Africa has not yet joined the 1965 Washington Convention on the Settlement of Investment Disputes between States and Nationals of Other States (ICSID).[647]

266. The proposed Draft International Arbitration Bill was designed to give fuller effect to South Africa's treaty obligations under the New York Convention.[648] However, the law reform proposals of the SALC have not been adopted. The Constitutional Court has taken a bold first step to modernize the law on referring disputes to arbitration in *Lufuno Mphaphuli & Associates (Pty) Ltd v. Andrews and*

642. Edwards & Kahn *LAWSA: Conflict*, para. 350; Forsyth *Private International Law*, 452.
643. Edwards & Kahn *LAWSA: Conflict*, para. 351; Forsyth *Private International Law*, 454; Spiro *Parent and Child*, 498–499.
644. 40 of 1977.
645. Sections 2 and 3.
646. Section 4(1)(b).
647. 575 *UNTS* 159. See Roodt 2004 (2) *Codicillus* 70.
648. South African Law Commission: Report on Domestic Arbitration (Project 94). For a discussion of the shortcomings of the Recognition and Enforcement of Foreign Arbitral Awards Act 40 of 1977, as well as the implications of the proposed new International Arbitration Act of 2000, see Van Niekerk and Schulze *International Trade*, 347ff.

Another.[649] Although the case did not contain an international element, the comparative law approach, adopted by the court included a reference to the UNCITRAL Model Law on International Commercial Arbitration, the recommendations for law reform made by the SALC, and the English Arbitration Act 1996. The judiciary has 'taken the lead' in an area where the legislature has chosen to remain passive. This guidance could be significant for international commercial arbitration in future.[650]

649. *Lufuno Mphaphuli & Associates (Pty) Ltd v. Andrews and Another* [2009] ZACC 6.
650. Roodt 2011 *CILSA* 323, 338.

Selected Bibliography

Authoritative Works and Mode of Citation

Allen, C.K. 'Status and Capacity'. *LQR* (1930): 277. Cited as: Allen, 1930 *LQR* 277.

Anton, A.E. *Private International Law.* 2nd edn. W. Green: Edinburgh, 1990. Cited as: Anton *Private International Law.*

Barrie, G. 'The Approach of the Courts Regarding South African Custodial Parents Going into the Diaspora'. *TSAR* (2009): 562. Cited as: Barrie 2009 *TSAR* 562.

Beck, A. 'The Convenience of Jurisdiction'. *SALJ* (1983): 43. Cited as: Beck 1983 *SALJ* 43.

Beckett, W.E. 'The Question of Classification in Private International Law'. *BYBIL* (1934): 46. Cited as: Beckett 1934 *BYBIL* 46.

Bennett, T.W. 'Choice of Law Rules in Claims of Unjust Enrichment'. *ICLQ* (1990): 136. Cited as: Bennett 1990 *ICLQ* 136.

Bennett, T.W. *Customary Law in South Africa.* Juta: Lansdowne, 2004. Cited as: Bennett *Customary Law.*

Bennet, T.W. & Kopke, K. 'Characterization and "Gap" in the Conflict of Laws'. *SALJ* (2008): 62. Cited as: Bennet and Kopke 2008 *SALJ* 62.

Binchy, W. *Irish Conflicts of Law.* Butterworths: Ireland, 1988. Cited as: Binchy *Irish Conflicts.*

Boberg, P.Q.R. 'Sharing Matrimonial Assets'. *BML* (1987): 80. Cited as: Boberg 1987 *BML* 80.

Calitz, K. 'The Jurisdiction of the Labour Court in International Employment Contracts in respect of Workplaces outside South Africa'. *Obiter* (2011): 678. Cited as Calitz 2011 *Obiter* 678.

Castel, J.G. & J. Walker. *Canadian Conflict of Laws.* 5th edn. Butterworths: Toronto, 2002. Cited as: Castel *Canadian Conflict.*

'Conflict of Laws', 1947–2005 *ASSAL* Juta: Cape Town, Wynberg, Johannesburg, 1948–1998. Cited as: *ASSAL* 1947–2005.

Corbett, M.M. 'The Zambian Trust: An Opinion Revisited'. *TSAR* (1993): 1. Cited as: Corbett 1993 *TSAR* 1.

Corbett, M.M., G. Hofmeyr & E. Kahn. *The Law of Succession in South Africa.* 2nd edn, Juta Law: Lansdowne, 2001. Cited as: Corbett, Hofmeyr Kahn *Succession.*

Corbett, M.M., H.R. Hahlo & G. Hofmeyr. *The Law of Succession in South Africa* with an *Appendix on the Conflict of Laws* by E. Kahn Juta: Cape Town, Wetton, Johannesburg, 1980. Cited as: Kahn *Appendix: Succession.*

Selected Bibliography

Cook, W.W. *The Logical and Legal Bases of the Conflict of Laws.* Cambridge, Massachusetts: Harvard University Press, 1949. Cited as: Cook *Logical and Legal Bases.*

Corpus Iuris Civilis Iustinianei Lugduni, 1627 reprinted by Otto Zeller: Osnabrück, 1965 (Translation of the whole *Corpus Iuris Civilis* by S.P. Scott *The Civil Law*). The Central Trust Company: Cincinnati, 1932; Translation of the *Digest* by Mommsen, T., P. Krueger & A. Watson. *The Digest of Justinian.* Philadelphia: University of Pennsylvania Press, 1985). Cited as: *Corpus Iuris Civilis.*

Crawford, J.R. 'The "Proper" Law of a Delict'. *SALJ* (1968): 314. Cited as: Crawford 1968 *SALJ* 314.

De Jager, F.J. *Domicilium as Koppelfaktor in die Internasionale Privaatreg.* Pretoria: (LLM Dissertation) University of South Africa, 1973. Cited as: De Jager *Domicilium as Koppelfaktor.*

De Nova, R. 'Current Developments of Private International Law'. *Am J Comp L* (1964): 542. Cited as: De Nova 1964 *Am J Comp L* 542.

De Vos, W. *Verrykingsaanspreeklikheid in die Suid-Afrikaanse Reg.* 3rd edn. Cape Town, Wetton, Johannesburg: Juta, 1987. Cited as: De Vos *Verrykingsaanspreeklikheid.*

De Winter, L.I. 'Nationality or Domicile?': The Present State of Affairs'. *Hague Recueil* III (1969): 349. Cited as: De Winter 1969 III *Hague Recueil* 349.

Dicey, A.V. *A Digest of the Law of England with Reference to the Conflict of Laws.* London: Stevens, 1896. Cited as: Dicey *Digest.*

Dicey, Morris & Collins. *The Conflict of Laws Vol. 1 and Vol. 2.* 14th edn. London: Sweet & Maxwell, 2006. Cited as: *Dicey-Morris Vol. 1 or Vol. 2.*

Du Plessis, S.J. 'Die Suid-Afrikaanse Internasionale Deliktereg'. In *Gedenkbundel HL Swanepoel.* Edited by J.A. Coetzee. Durban: Butterworths, 1976. Cited as: Du Plessis *Gedenkbundel.*

Du Toit, S.J. 'International Funds Transfers and Private International Law'. *SA Merc LJ* (2006): 53. Cited as: Du Toit 2006 *SA Merc LJ* 53.

Edwards, A.B. 'Choice of Law in Delict: Rules or Approach?'. *SALJ* (1979): 48. Cited as: Edwards 1979 *SALJ* 48.

Edwards, A.B. 'Some Reflections on the Reception of the "Proper Law" Doctrine into South African Law'. In *Huldigingsbundel Paul van Warmelo.* edited by J. Van der Westhuizen et al. Pretoria: University of South Africa, 1984. Cited as: Edwards *Huldigingsbundel.*

Edwards, A.B. 'Locus Regit Actum'. *THRHR* (1986): 144. Cited as: Edwards 1986 *THRHR* 144.

Edwards, A.B. updated by Kahn, E., Title on *Conflict of Laws* in Vol. 2, Part 2 (2nd ed.) of Joubert, W.A. *The Law of South Africa.* Durban: LexisNexis Butterworths, 2003. Cited as: Edwards & Kahn *LAWSA: Conflict.*

Ehrenzweig, A. 'The not so "Proper Law" of a Tort: Pandora's Box'. *ICLQ* (1968): 1. Cited as: Ehrenzweig 1968 *ICLQ* 1.

Eiselen, S. 'International Jurisdiction in Claims Sounding in Money'. *SA Merc LJ* (2006): 45. Cited as: Eiselen 2006 *SA Merc LJ* 45.

Eiselen, S. '*Laconian* Revisited – A Reappraisal of Classification in Conflicts Law'. *SALJ* (2006): 146. Cited as: Eiselen 2006 *SALJ* 146.

Eiselen, S. 'Goodbye Arrest *ad Fundandam*. Hello *Forum non Conveniens*?'. *TSAR* (2008): 794. Cited as: Eiselen 2008 *TSAR* 794.

Falconbridge, J.D. *Essays on the Conflict of Laws*. 2nd edn. Toronto: Canada Law Book Company, 1954. Cited as: Falconbridge *Conflict*.

Fawcett, J.J. 'Result Selection in Domicile Cases'. *Oxford Jour Leg Stud* (1985): 378. Cited as: Fawcett 1985 *Oxford Jour Leg Stud* 378.

Fawcett, J.J. 'The Interrelationships of Jurisdiction and Choice of Law in Private International Law'. *Current Legal Problems* (1991): 39. Cited as: Fawcett 1991 *Current Legal Problems* 39.

Forsyth, C. 'Enforcement of Arbitral Awards, Choice of Law in Contract, Characterisation and a New Attitude to Private International Law'. *SALJ* (1987): 4. Cited as: Forsyth 1987 *SALJ* 4.

Forsyth, C.F. *Private International Law*. 5th edn. Cape Town, Wetton, Johannesburg: Juta, 2012. Cited as: Forsyth *Private International Law*.

Forsyth, C. '"Mind the Gap": A Practical Example of the Characterisation of Prescription/Limitation Rules'. *Journal of Private International Law* (2006): 169. Cited as: Forsyth 2006 *Journal of Private International Law*, 169.

Forsyth, C. '"Mind the Gap Part II": The South African Supreme Court of Appeal and Characterisation'. *Journal of Private International Law* (2006): 425. Cited as: Forsyth 2006 *Journal of Private International Law*, 425.

Forsyth, C.F. 'The Impact of the Domestic on the International: Some Crucial Deficiencies in the South African Law of Jurisdiction with their Regional and International Consequences'. *SA Merc LJ* (2006): 1. Cited as: Forsyth 2006 *SA Merc LJ* 1.

Frames, G.C. 'Domicil'. *Cape LJ* (1884): 253. Cited as: Frames 1884 *Cape LJ* 253.

Fredericks, E.A. & J.L. Neels. 'The Proper Law of a Documentary Letter of Credit'. 2003 *SA Merc LJ* 63; 205. Cited as: Fredericks & Neels 2003 *SA Merc LJ*.

Fredericks, E.A. 'The Proper Law of the International Contract of Employment: Interpreting the *Kleinhans* Case'. *SA Merc LJ* (2006): 75. Cited as: Fredericks 2006 *SA Merc LJ*.

Fredericks, E.A. 'Contractual Capacity in Private International Law: Interpreting the *Powell* Case'. *THRHR* (2006): 279. Cited as: Fredericks 2006 *THRHR* 279.

Graveson, R.H. *Conflict of Laws*. 7th edn. London: Sweet & Maxwell, 1974. Cited as: Graveson *Conflict*.

Guttman, E. 'The Status of Legitimacy in Comparative Conflict of Laws'. *ICLQ* (1959): 678. Cited as: Guttman 1959 *ICLQ* 678.

Hahlo, H.R. & E. Kahn. *The Union of South Africa: The Development of its Laws and Constitution*. London, Cape Town: Stevens & Juta, 1960. Cited as: Hahlo & Kahn *Union*.

Hahlo, H.R. & E. Kahn. *The South African Law of Husband and Wife* with an appendix by Kahn, E. on *Jurisdiction and Conflict of Laws*. 4th edn. Cape Town, Wynberg, Johannesburg: Juta, 1972. Cited as: Hahlo & Kahn *Husband and Wife*.

Hahlo, H.R. & E. Kahn. *The South African Legal System and its Background*. Cape Town, Wynberg, Johannesburg: Juta, 1973. Cited as: Hahlo & Kahn *South African Legal System*.

Hall, C. '*Cruse v. Chittum*: Habitual Residence Judicially Explored'. *ICLQ* (1975): 1. Cited as: Hall 1975 *ICLQ* 1.

Hall, C.G. *Maasdorp's Institutes of South African Law*, Vol. II *The Law of Property.* 10th edn. Cape Town, Wynberg, Johannesburg: Juta, 1976. Cited as: Hall *Maasdorp's Institutes.*

Harms, L.T.C. *Civil Procedure in the Superior Courts.* Durban: LexisNexis Butterworths, 2003. Cited as: Harms *Civil Procedure.*

Heaton, J. & E. Schoeman. 'Foreign Marriages and Section 7(3) of the Divorce Act 70 of 1979: *Esterhuizen v. Esterhuizen* 1999 (1) SA 492(C)'. *THRHR* (2000): 141. Cited as: Heaton & Schoeman 2000 *THRHR* 141.

Hosten, W.J. et al., *Introduction to South African Law and Legal Theory.* 2nd edn. Durban: Butterworths, 1997. Cited as: Hosten, Edwards, Bosman & Church *Introduction.*

Huber, U. *De Conflictu Legum Diversarum in Diversis Imperiis*, a chapter in Huber's *Praelectiones Juris Civilis* (Franeker 1687). Copies of the text of *De Conflictu Legum* are to be found in Lorenzen, E.G. *Selected Articles on the Conflict of Laws.* New Haven: Yale University Press, 1947; London: Oxford University Press, 1947, which also contains an English translation of the Latin text, and Von Savigny, F.C. *Private International Law, and the Retrospective Operation of Statutes: A Treatise on the Conflict of Laws and the Limits in Respect of Place and Time.* (translated by Guthrie, W. (2nd ed.) T. & T. Clark: Edinburgh; Stevens & Sons: London, 1880). Cited as: Huber *De Conflictu Legum.*

Kahn, E. 'Delict in the Conflict of Laws'. *SALJ* (1950): 66. Cited as: Kahn 1950 *SALJ* 66.

Kahn, E. 'The Law Determining Legitimacy'. *SALJ* (1955): 24. Cited as: Kahn 1955 *SALJ* 24.

Kahn, E. *The South African Law of Domicile of Natural Persons.* Cape Town, Wynberg, Johannesburg: Juta, 1972. Cited as: Kahn *Domicile.*

Kahn, E. 'Reform of the Law of Domicile: Time for Some History'. *TR* (1987): 113. Cited as: Kahn 1987 *TR* 113.

Kahn, E. 'International Contracts'. *BML* (1990–1991): 203 (I–VI). Cited as: Kahn 1990–1991 *BML* (I–VI).

Kahn-Freund, O. *General Problems of Private International Law.* Leiden: A.W. Sijthoff, 1976. Cited as: Kahn-Freund *General Problems.*

Kiggundu, J. 'Choice of Law in Delict: The Rise and Rise of the *Lex Loci Delicti Commissi*'. *SA Merc LJ* (2006): 97. Cited as: Kiggundu 2006 *SA Merc LJ* 97.

Lederman, W.R. 'Classification in Private International Law'. *Can B Rev* (1951): 3; 168. Cited as: Lederman 1951 *Can B Rev* 3; 168.

Lorenzen, E.G. *Selected Articles on the Conflict of Laws.* New Haven: Yale University Press, 1947; London: Oxford University Press, 1947. Cited as: Lorenzen.

Lupton, M. 'Divorce and Property Rights'. *BML* (1988): 119. Cited as: Lupton 1988 *BML* 119.

McClean, J.D. 'The Meaning of Residence'. *ICLQ* (1962): 1153. Cited as: McClean 1962 *ICLQ* 1153.

McClean, D. '*De Conflictu Legum*: Perspectives on Private International Law at the Turn of the Century'. *Recueil des Cours* 282 (2000): 41.

McClean, J.D. & V.R. Abou-Nigm. *Morris: The Conflict of Laws.* 8th edn. London: Sweet & Maxwell, 2012. Cited as: Morris *Conflict.*

Morse, J. 'Characterization: Shadow or Substance'. *Columbia LR* (1949): 1027. Cited as: Morse 1949 *Columbia LR* 1027.

Neels, J. 'Die *Lex Causae* vir Eiendomsoordrag van *Res in Transitu*'. *TSAR* (1991): 309. Cited as: Neels 1991 *TSAR* 309.

Neels, J.L. 'Die Internasionale Privaatreg en die Herverdelingsbevoegdheid by Egskeiding'. *TSAR* (1992): 336. Cited as: Neels 1992 *TSAR* 336.

Neels, J. 'Die Gedeeltelike Uitsluiting van *Renvoi* in Resente Wetgewing'. *TSAR* (1992): 739. Cited as: Neels 1992 *TSAR* 739.

Neels, J. 'Die Onegte Insidentele Vraag in 'n Internasionaal-Erfregtelike Geskil'. *TSAR* (1993): 760. Cited as: Neels 1993 *TSAR* 760.

Neels, J.L. 'Recent Developments in Private International Law 1993–2000'. paper delivered at RAU Legal Update on 30 November 2000 available at <general.rau.ac.za/law/English/ipr/1993–2000.DOC>. Cited as: Neels 1993–2000.

Neels, J.L. 'Recent Developments in Private International Law 2001–2002'. paper delivered at RAU Legal Update on 19 July 2002 available at <general.rau.ac.za/law/English/ipr/2001–2002.doc>. Cited as: Neels 2001–2002.

Neels, J.L. 'Substantiewe Geregtigheid, Herverdeling en Begunstiging in die Internasionale Familiereg'. *TSAR* (2001): 692. Cited as: Neels 2001 *TSAR* 692.

Neels, J.L. 'Classification as an Argumentative Device in International Family Law'. *SALJ* (2003): 883. Cited as: Neels 2003 *SALJ* 883.

Neels, J.L. 'The Proprietary Effect of Reservation-of-Title Clauses in Private International Law'. *SA Merc LJ* (2006): 66. Cited as Neels 2006 *SA Merc LJ* 66.

Neels, J.L. 'Revocation of Wills in South African Private International Law'. *ICLQ* (2007): 613. Cited as: Neels 2007 *ICLQ* 613.

Neels, J.L. 'Tweevoudige Leemte: Bevrydende Verjaring en die Internasionale Privaatreg'. *TSAR* (2007): 178. Cited as: Neels 2007 *TSAR* 178.

Neels, J.L. & E.A. Fredericks. 'The Music Performance Contract in European and South African Private International Law'. *THRHR* (2008): 529. Cited as: Neels & Fredericks 2008 *THRHR* 529.

Neels, J.L. & M. Wethmar-Lemmer. 'Constitutional Values and the Proprietary Consequences of Marriage in Private International Law'. *TSAR* (2008): 587. Cited as: Neels & Wethmar-Lemmer 2008 *TSAR* 587.

Neels, J.L. 'Falconbridge in Africa'. *JPIL* (2008): 167. Cited as: Neels 2008 *JPIL* 167.

Neels, J.L. 'Consumer Protection and Private International Law'. *Obiter* (2010): 122. Cited as: Neels 2010 *Obiter* 122.

Neels, J.L. 'External Public Policy, the Incidental Question Properly So-called and the Recognition of Foreign Divorce Orders'. *TSAR* (2010): 671. Cited as: Neels 2010 *TSAR* 671.

Neels, J.L. & E.A. Fredericks. 'Tacit Choice of Law in the Hague Principles on Choice of Law in International Contracts'. *De Jure* (2011): 101. Cited as: Neels & Fredericks 2011 *De Jure* 101.

Neuhaus, P.H. *Die Grundbegriffe des Internationalen Privatrechts.* 2nd edn. Tübingen: JCB Mohr (Paul Siebeck), 1976. Cited as: Neuhaus *Grundbegriffe*.

North, P.M. & J.J. Fawcett. *Cheshire and North's Private International Law.* 13th edn. London, Dublin, Edinburgh: Butterworths, 1999; Fawcett, J.J. & J.M. Carruthers. *Cheshire, North and Fawcett: Private Internatiaonal Law.* 14th edn. Oxford: Oxford University Press, 2008. Cited as: *Cheshire-North.*

Nygh, P.E. 'The Reception of Domicile into English Private International Law'. *Tasm ULR* (1961): 555. Cited as: Nygh 1961 *Tasm ULR* 555.

Nygh, P.E. 'Foreign Status, Public Policy and Discretion'. *ICLQ* (1964): 39. Cited as: Nygh 1964 *ICLQ* 39.

Nygh, P.E. & M. Davis. *Conflict of Laws in Australia.* 7th edn. Sydney, Brisbane, Melbourne, Adelaide, Canberra, Perth: Butterworths, 2002. Cited as: Nygh *Conflict.*

Oppong, R.F. 'Roman-Dutch Law Meets Common Law on Jurisdiction in International Matters'. *JPIL* (2008): 311. Cited as: Oppong 2008 *JPIL* 311.

Pålsson, L. *Marriage and Divorce in Comparative Conflict of Laws.* Leiden: A.W. Sijthoff, 1974. Cited as: Pålsson *Marriage and Divorce.*

Pollak, W. *The South African Law of Jurisdiction.* Johannesburg: Hortors, 1937. Cited as: Pollak *Jurisdiction.*

Pryles, M. 'The Basis of Adjudicatory Competence in Private International Law'. *ICLQ* (1972): 61. Cited as: Pryles 1972 *ICLQ* 61.

Rabel, E. *The Conflict of Laws: A Comparative Study.* 2nd edn. Ann Arbor: University of Michigan Law School, 1958. Cited as: Rabel *Conflict: Comparative.*

Ranchod, B.G. 'The Concept of Domicile in South African Law'. *Acta Juridica* (1970): 53. Cited as: Ranchod 1970 *Acta Juridica* 53.

Robertson, A.H. *Characterization in the Conflict of Laws.* (Harvard Studies on the Conflict of Laws), Cambridge, Massachusetts: Harvard University Press, 1940. Cited as: Robertson *Characterization.*

Roodt, H.C. 'Migrerende Egpare se Huweliksgoedere-probleme: *Common Law* en Gemengde Stelsels'. *THRHR* (1995): 194; 440. Cited as: Roodt 1995 *THRHR* 194; 440.

Roodt, H.C. 'The Integration of Substantive Interests and Material Justice in South African Choice of Law'. *CILSA* (2003): 1. Cited as: Roodt 2003 *CILSA* 1.

Roodt, H.C. 'Jurisdiction of the South African Labour Court: Employer Identity and Party Autonomy'. *SA Mercantile Law Journal* 15 (2003): 135–149. Cited as: Roodt 2003 *SA Merc LJ.*

Roodt, H.C. 'The Recognition and Enforcement of Foreign Judgments, Maintenance Orders and Arbitral Awards: A Proposal for Structural Reform'. *Codicillus* 2 (2004): 64. Cited as: Roodt 2004 (2) *Codicillus* 64.

Roodt, H.C. 'Recognition and Enforcement of Foreign Judgments: Still a Hobson's Choice Among Competing Theories?'. *CILSA* (2005): 15. Cited as: Roodt 2005 *CILSA* 15.

Roodt, H.C. 'Conflict of Laws as a Tool in the Trade of Works of Art'. *TSAR* (2005): 690. Cited as: Roodt 2005 *TSAR* 690.

Roodt, H.C. 'Conflict of Law(s) and Autonomy in Antenuptial Agreements (Part 1, 2 and 3)'. *Tydskrif vir Hedendaagse Romeins-Hollandse Reg* (2006): 215; 367 and 546. Cited as: Roodt 2006 *THRHR* 215; 367 or 546 respectively.

Roodt, H.C. 'Reflections on Theory, Doctrine and Method in Choice of Law'. *CILSA* (2007): 77 Cited as: Roodt 2007 *CILSA* 77.

Roodt, H.C. 'A Wider Vision in Choice of Prescription Law'. *Yearbook of Private International Law* (2007): 357. Cited as: Roodt 2007 *Yearbook* 357.

Roodt, H.C. 'Recognition of Muslim Marriages in South Africa: A Conflicts Perspective'. *The International Journal of Diversity in Organisations, Communications and Nations* (2008): 137. Cited as: Roodt 2008 *International Journal of Diversity* 137.

Roodt, H.C. 'Autonomy and Due Process in Arbitration: Recalibrating the Balance'. *Comparative and International Law Journal for Southern Africa* (2011): 311. Cited as: Roodt 2011 *CILSA* 311.

Schoeman, E. 'Wesenlike Geldigheid van die Huwelik in die Internasionale Privaatreg'. *Codicillus* 1 (1992): 22. Cited as: Schoeman 1992 (1) *Codicillus* 22.

Schoeman, E. 'Die Herkoms en Ontwikkeling van *Domicilium* as Verbindingsfaktor in Internasionale Privaatreg'. *THRHR* (1994): 204. Cited as: Schoeman 1994 *THRHR* 204.

Schoeman, E. 'The Abolition of the Wife's Domicile of Dependency: A Lesson in History'. *THRHR* (1995): 488. Cited as: Schoeman 1995 *THRHR* 488.

Schoeman, E. *Domicile and Jurisdiction as Criteria in External Conflict of Laws with Particular Reference to the South African Law of Persons* (Doctoral Thesis). Pretoria: University of South Africa, 1997. Cited as: Schoeman *Domicile.*

Schoeman, E. 'Domicile, Status and Divorce in South African Conflict of Laws: A Historical Perspective'. *Fundamina* 4 (1998): 1. Cited as: Schoeman 1998 (4) *Fundamina* 1.

Schoeman, E. 'Choice of Law and Legitimacy: Back to 1917?'. *SALJ* (1999): 288. Cited as: Schoeman 1999 *SALJ* 288.

Schoeman, E. 'The Connecting Factor for the Proprietary Consequences of Marriage'. *TSAR* (2001): 72. Cited as Schoeman 2001 *TSAR* 72.

Schulze, C. 'Conflicting Law of Conflict in Cases of International Succession'. *CILSA* (2001): 34. Cited as: Schulze 2001 *CILSA* 34.

Schulze, C. 'Practical Problems Regarding the Enforcement of Foreign Money Judgments'. *SA Merc LJ* (2005): 125. Cited as: Schulze 2005 *SA Merc LJ* 125.

Schulze, C. *On Jurisdiction and the Recognition and Enforcement of Foreign Money Judgments*. Pretoria: University of South Africa Press, 2005. Cited as: Schulze *On Jurisdiction.*

Schulze, C. 'Electronic Commerce and Civil Jurisdiction, with Special Reference to Consumer Contracts'. *SA Merc LJ* (2006): 31. Cited as: Schulze 2006 *SA Merc LJ* 31.

Schulze, C. 'Formalistic and Discretionary Approaches to Characterization in Private International Law'. *SALJ* (2006): 161. Cited as: 2006 *SALJ* 161.

Schulze, C. 'International Jurisdiction in Claims Sounding in Money: is *Richman v. Ben-Tovim* the Last Word?'. *SA Merc LJ* (2008): 61. Cited as: Schulze 2008 *SA Merc LJ* 61.

Schulze, C. 'Conflict of Laws'. *Annual Survey of South African Law* (2008): 167. Cited as: Schulze 2008 *Annual Survey* 167.

Schulze, C. 'Conflict of Laws'. *Annual Survey of South African Law* (2009): 134. Cited as: Schulze 2009 *Annual Survey* 134.

Schulze, C. 'Conflict of Laws'. *Annual Survey of South African Law* (2010): 179. Cited as: Schulze 2010 *Annual Survey* 179.

Schuz, R. *A Modern Approach to the Incidental Question.* Kluwer Law International, 1997. Cited as: Schuz *Incidental Question.*
Silberberg, H. *The Recognition and Enforcement of Foreign Judgments in South Africa.* Pretoria: Institute for Foreign and Comparative Law (University of South Africa), 1973. Cited as: Silberberg *Foreign Judgments.*
Sinclair, J. (assisted by J. Heaton). *The Law of Marriage.* (Vol. I) Cape Town: Juta, 1996. Cited as: Sinclair *Law of Marriage.*
Smit, H. 'Common and Civil Law Rules of *In Personam* Adjudicatory Authority: An Analysis of Underlying Policies'. *ICLQ* (1972): 335. Cited as: Smit 1972 *ICLQ* 335.
Spiro, E. *Conflict of Laws.* Cape Town, Wynberg, Johannesburg, Durban: Juta, 1973. Cited as: Spiro *Conflict.*
Spiro, E. *Law of Parent and Child.* 4th edn, Cape Town, Wetton, Johannesburg: Juta 1985. Cited as: Spiro *Parent and Child.*
Spiro, E. 'Conflict of the *Locus Regit Actum* Rule and the *Lex Causae*'. *THRHR* (1986): 139. Cited as: Spiro 1986 *THRHR* 139.
Stoll, H. & P.J. Visser. 'Aspects of the Reform of German (and South African) Private International Family Law'. *De Jure* (1989): 330. Cited as: Stoll & Visser 1989 *De Jure* 330.
Story, J. *Commentaries on the Conflict of Laws.* 8th edn. by Bigelow M.M. Boston: Little, Brown and Co, 1883. Cited as: Story *Commentaries.*
Suijling, J.P. *De Statutentheorie in Nederland gedurende de XVIIde Eeuw.* s-Hertogenbosch: (LL.D. Thesis, Rijks University), Firma Robijns & Co, 1893. Cited as: Suijling *Statutentheorie.*
Terblanche, P. '*Lex Fori* or *Lex Loci Delicti*? The Problem of Choice of Law in International Delicts'. *CILSA* (1997): 243. Cited as: Terblanche 1997 *CILSA* 243.
Thomashausen, A.E.A.M. 'Reflections on "Domicile" as a Connecting Factor'. In *Huldigingsbundel vir WA Joubert.* Durban: Butterworths, 1988. Cited as: Thomashausen *Reflections on 'Domicile'.*
Thomashausen, A.E.A.M. 'The Enforcement and Recognition of Judgments and other Forms of Legal Cooperation in the SADC'. *CILSA* (2002): 26. Cited as: Thomashausen 2002 *CILSA* 26.
Turpin. 'Characterisation and Policy in the Conflict of Laws'. *Acta Juridica* (1959): 222. Cited as: Turpin 1959 *Acta Juridica* 22.
Van Niekerk, J.P. & Schulze, W.G. *The South African Law of International Trade: Selected Topics.* 3rd edn. Pretoria: SAGA Legal Publications CC, 2011. Cited as: Van Niekerk & Schulze *International Trade.*
Van Niekerk, J.P. 'Choice of Foreign Law in a South African Marine Insurance Policy: An Unjustified Limitation of Party Autonomy?'. *TSAR* (2011): 159. Cited as Van Niekerk 2011 *TSAR* 159.
Van Rooyen, J.C.W. *Die Kontrak in die Suid-Afrikaanse Internasionale Privaatreg.* Kaapstad, Wynberg, Johannesburg: Juta, 1972. Cited as: Van Rooyen *Kontrak.*
Van Schalkwyk, L.N. 'Artikel 7(3) van die Wet op Egskeiding 70 van 1979 – Toepassing by Lompsom as Onderhoudsbevel'. *TSAR* (1999): 378. Cited as: Van Schalkwyk 1999 *TSAR* 378.

Van Zyl, D.H. *Geskiedenis van die Romeins-Hollandse Reg.* Durban: Butterworths, 1979. Cited as: Van Zyl *Geskiedenis.*

Visser, C. 'Choice of Law in Internet Copyright Disputes'. *SA Merc LJ* (1999): 268. Cited as: Visser 1999 *SA Merc LJ* 268.

Visser, P.J. 'Enkele Gedagtes oor Fundamentele Regte en die Familiereg'. *THRHR* (1995): 702. Cited as: Visser 1995 *THRHR* 702.

Voet, J. *Commentarius ad Pandectas.* Hagae-Comitum, 1698–1704 (Translation by Gane P. *The Selective Voet, being the Commentary on the Pandects.* Durban: Butterworths, 1955). Cited as: Voet *Commentarius.*

Von Bar, L. *The Theory and Practice of Private International Law.* (translated by Gillespie G.R.). 2nd edn. Edinburgh: William Green & Sons Law Publishers, 1892. Cited as: Von Bar *Theory and Practice.*

Von Mehren, A.T. & D.T. Trautman. 'Jurisdiction to Adjudicate: A Suggested Analysis'. *Harv LR* (1966): 1121. Cited as: Von Mehren & Trautman 1966 *Harv LR* 1121.

Von Savigny, F.C. *Private International Law, and the Retrospective Operation of Statutes: A Treatise on the Conflict of Laws and the Limits in Respect of Place and Time.* (translated by Guthrie, W.). 2nd edn. T. & T. Clark: Edinburgh; London: Stevens & Sons, 1880. Cited as: Von Savigny *Private International Law.*

Vrancken, P.H.G. 'Foreign Informal Antenuptial Contracts and S 7(3) of the Divorce Act 70 of 1979'. *TSAR* (1993) 180. Cited as: Vrancken 1993 *TSAR* 180.

Westlake, J. *Treatise on Private International Law.* 3rd edn. London: Sweet and Maxwell, 1890. Cited as: Westlake *Treatise.*

Wethmar-Lemmer M. 'When Could a South African Court be Expected to Apply the United Nations Convention on Contracts for the International Sale of Goods?'. *De Jure* (2008): 419. Cited as: Wethmar-Lemmer 2008 *De Jure* 419.

Welsh, R.S. 'Legitimacy in the Conflict of Laws'. *LQR* (1947): 65. Cited as: Welsh 1947 *LQR* 65.

Yntema, H.E. 'The Historic Bases of Private International Law'. In *Selected Readings on Conflict of Laws.* St Paul, Minnesota: West Publishing Co., 1956. Cited as: Yntema *Historic Bases.*

Cases

South African

AS v. CS 2011 (2) SA 360 (WCC).

Anderson v. The Master 1949 (4) SA 660 (E).

Amod v. Multilateral Motor Vehicle Accident Fund 1999 (4) SA 1319 (SCA).

Aspeling NO v. Alexander 1919 AD 139.

Astral Operations (Ltd) v. Parry (2008) 29 ILJ 2668 (LAC).

Bell v. Bell, 1991 (4) SA 195 (W).

Benidai Trading Co. Ltd. v. Gouws and Gouws 1977 (3) SA 1020 (T).

Bid Industrial Holdings (Pty) Ltd v. Strang 2008 (3) SA 355 (SCA).

Blatchford v. Blatchford's Executors (1881) 1 EDC 365.

Bisonboard Ltd. v. K Braun Woodworking Machinery (Pty) Ltd. 1991 (1) SA 482 (A).

Selected Bibliography

Bominflot Ltd. v. Kien Hung Shipping Co. Ltd. (Central Leasing Corporation & another Intervening), 2004 (2) SA 556 (C).
Brown v. Brown 1921 AD 478.
Burchell v. Anglin 2010 (3) SA 48 (ECG).
C Hoare and Co. v. Runewitsch and Another 1997 (1) SA 338 (W).
Consolidated Estates and Trusts Ltd. v. Turnbull, 1924 TPD 1.
Creutzburg & another v. Commercial Bank of Namibia Ltd. [2006] 4 All SA 327 (SCA).
Daniels v. Campbell NO and Others 2004 (7) BCLR 735 (CC); 2004 (5) SA 331 (CC).
Donelly, Ex Parte 1915 WLD 29.
Estate Agents Board v. Lek 1979 (3) SA 1048 (A).
Esterhuizen v. Esterhuizen 1999 (1) SA 492 (C).
Ewing McDonald & Co. Ltd. v. M & M Products Co. Ltd. 1991 (1) SA 252 (A).
Ferraz v. D'Inhaca 1904 TH 137.
Frankel's Estate and Another v. The Master and Another 1950 (1) SA 220 (A).
Friedman v. Friedman's Executors and Others (1922) 43 NLR 259.
Gaarn v. Cairn's Executors 1910 EDL 462.
Gilbert v. Gilbert (1901) 22 NLR 201.
Govu v. Stuart (1903) 24 NLR 440.
Guggenheim v. Rosenbaum (2) 1961 (4) SA 21 (W).
Haines v. Haines, Unreported, Case No. 1683/1991.
Hamburg v. Pickard 1906 TS 1010 (PC).
Hamid v. Minister of the Interior 1954 (4) SA 241 (T).
Harnischfeger Corporation and Another v. Appleton and Another 1993 (4) SA 479 (W).
Hassam v. Jacobs NO and Others 2008 (4) All SA 360 (C); 2009 (5) SA 572 (CC).
Hassan v. Hassan 1998 (2) SA 589 (D) 589.
Herbst v. Surti 1991 (2) SA 75 (Z).
Holland v. Holland 1973 (1) SA 897 (T).
Holz v. Harksen 1995 (3) SA 521 (C).
Hugo v. Wessels 1987 (3) SA 837 (A).
Hulscher v. Voorschotkas voor Zuid-Afrika 1908 TS 542.
Improvair (Cape) (Pty) Ltd. v. Establissements Neu 1983 (2) SA 138 (C).
ISM Inter Ltd. v. Maraldo and Another 1983 (4) SA 112 (T).
Ismail v. Ismail 1983 (1) SA 1006 (A).
Johnson v. Johnson 1931 AD 391.
Jones: In Re Jones v. Jones, Ex Parte 1984 (4) SA 725 (W).
Jones v. Krok 1995 (1) SA 677 (A).
Kaiser, Ex Parte 1902 TH 165.
Kassim v. Ghumran and Another 1981 (4) SA 79 (Z).
Kent v. Salmon 1910 TPD 637.
Kleinhans v. Parmalat SA (Pty) Ltd. [2002] 9 BLLR 879 (LC).
Kuhne and Nagel AG Zürich v. APA Distributors (Pty) Ltd. 1981 (3) SA 536 (W).
Laconian Maritime Enterprises Ltd. v. Agromar Lineas Ltd. 1986 (3) SA 509 (D).
Laurens v. Von Höhne 1993 (2) SA 104 (W).
Lewis v. Lewis 1939 WLD 140.

Lief NO v. Dettmann 1964 (2) SA 252 (A).
Lufuno Mphaphuli & Associates (Pty) Ltd v. Andrews and Another [2009] ZACC 6.
Mackay v. Philip (1830) 1 Menz 455.
Marcard Stein and Co. v. Port Marine Contractors (Pty) Ltd. 1995 (3) SA (A).
Mason v. Mason 1885 4 EDC 330.
Milbourn v. Milbourn 1987 (3) SA 62 (W).
Minister of Transport, Transkei v. Abdul 1995 (1) SA 366 (N).
Minister of Home Affairs v. Fourie (Doctors for Life International and Other, Amici Curiae); Lesbian and Gay Equality Project and Others v. Minister of Home Affairs 2006 (1) SA 524 (CC).
Ochberg v. Ochberg's Estate 1941 CPD 15.
Parry v. Astral Operations Ltd. [2005] 10 BLLR 989 (LC).
Perrot-Humphrey v. Perrot-Humphrey 1967 (3) SA 304 (W).
Pitluk v. Gavendo 1955 (2) SA 573 (T).
Powell v. Powell 1953 (4) SA 380 (W).
Pretorius v. Pretorius 1948 (4) SA 144 (O).
Purser v. Sales 2001 (3) SA 445 (SCA).
Reinhardt v. Ricker and David 1905 TS 179.
Representative of Lloyds and Others v. Classic Sailing Adventures (Pty) Ltd 2010 (5) SA 90 (SCA).
Richman v. Ben-Tovim 2007 (2) SA 283 (SCA).
Righetti v. Pinchin and Another 1955 (3) SA 338 (D).
Rogaly v. General Imports (Pty) Ltd. 1948 (1) SA 1216 (C).
Roux v. Kuils River Syndicate 1912 TPD 547.
Ryland v. Edros 1997 (2) SA 690 (C).
Sadiku v. Sadiku Unreported, Case No. 30498/06 (TPD).
Schlimmer v. Executrix in Estate of Rising 1904 TH 108.
Schmidt v. Weaving 2009 (1) SA 170 (SCA).
Seedat's Executors v. The Master (Natal) 1917 AD 302.
Society of Lloyd's v. Price and Lee 2005 (3) SA 549 (T).
Society of Lloyd's v. Price; Society of Lloyd's v. Lee [2006] JOL 17577 (SCA).
Society of Lloyd's v. Romahn 2006 (4) SA 23 (C).
Sperling v. Sperling 1975 (3) SA 707 (A).
Spinazze, Ex Parte and Another NNO 1985 (3) SA 650 (A).
Standard Bank of South Africa Ltd. v. Efroiken and Newman 1924 AD 171.
Standard Bank of SA Ltd. v. Ocean Commodities Inc. 1983 (1) SA 276 (A).
Standard Chartered Bank of Canada v. Nedperm Bank Ltd. 1994 (4) SA 747 (A).
Stewart v. Ryall (1887) 5 SC 146.
Steytler NO v. Fitzgerald 1911 AD 295.
Taylor, Ex Parte et Uxor 1949 (2) SA 254 (C).
Tesoriero v. Bhyjo Investments Share Block (Pty) Ltd. (R) 2000 (1) SA 167 (W).
Timms v. Nicol 1968 (1) SA 299 (R).
Tomlinson v. Zwirchmayr 1998 (2) SA 840 (T).
Union Government v. Fischer's Executrix 1921 TPD 328.
Van Borselen, Ex Parte et Uxor, 1942 TPD 206.
Van Dam, Ex Parte, 1973 (2) SA 182 (W).

Von Wintzingerode v. Von Wintzingerode 1964 (2) SA 618 (T).
Weatherley v. Weatherley (1879) Kotzé 66.

Foreign

Amin Rasheed Shipping Corp v. Kuwait Insurance Co. [1983] 2 All ER 884 (HL).
Babcock v. Jackson 191 NE 2d 279 (1963), 2 Lloyd's Rep 286.
Bonython v. Commonwealth of Australia 1951 AC 201.
Compagnie d'Armement SA v. Compagnie Tunisienne de Navigation SA [1971] 1 AC 572.
Forbes v. Forbes (1854) Kay 341, 69 ER 145.
Hodgson v. Beauchesne (1858) 12 Moo PCC 285, 14 ER 920.
Lord v. Colvin (1859) 4 Drew 366, 62 ER 141.
Munro v. Munro (1840) 7 Cl and Fin 842, HL, 7 ER 1288.
Pottinger v. Wightman (1817) 3 Mer 67, 36 ER 26.
Somerville v. Somerville (1801) 5 Ves 750, 31 ER 839.
Tzortzis v. Monarch Line A/B [1968] 1 All ER 949.
Udny v. Udny (1869) LR 1 Sc and Div 441.
Whicker v. Hume (1858) 7 HLC 124, 11 ER 50.
Winans v. Attorney-General [1904] AC 287.
Joined Cases C-509/09 and C-161/10 *eDate Advertising GmbH v. X and Olivier Martinez and Robert Martinez v. MGN Limited*

Statutes

Deeds Registries Act 47 of 1937.
Insurance Act 27 of 1943.
Prohibition of Mixed Marriages Act 55 of 1949.
Wills Act 7 of 1953.
Supreme Court Act 59 of 1959.
Marriage Act 25 of 1961.
Reciprocal Enforcement of Maintenance Orders Act 80 of 1963.
Bills of Exchange Act 34 of 1964.
Companies Act 61 of 1973.
Recognition and Enforcement of Foreign Arbitral Awards Act 40 of 1977.
Patents Act 57 of 1978.
Copyright Act 98 of 1978.
Protection of Businesses Act 99 of 1978.
Divorce Act 70 of 1979.
Child Care Act 74 of 1983.
Matrimonial Property Act 88 of 1984.
Immorality and Prohibition of Mixed Marriages Amendment Act 72 of 1985.
Carriage of Goods by Sea Act 1 of 1986.
Children's Status Act 82 of 1987.

Enforcement of Foreign Civil Judgments Act 32 of 1988.
Law of Evidence Amendment Act 45 of 1988.
Reciprocal Enforcement of Maintenance Orders (Countries in Africa) Act 6 of 1989.
Domicile Act 3 of 1992.
Births and Deaths Registration Act 51 of 1992.
South African Citizenship Act 88 of 1995.
Labour Relations Act 66 of 1995.
Hague Convention on the Civil Aspects of International Child Abduction Act 72 of 1996.
Constitution of the Republic of South Africa 108 of 1996.
Basic Conditions of Employment Act 75 of 1997.
Long-term Insurance Act 52 of 1998.
Short-term Insurance Act 53 of 1998.
Recognition of Customary Marriages Act 120 of 1998.
Sea Transport Documents Act 65 of 2000.
Electronic Communications and Transactions Act 25 of 2002.
National Credit Act 34 of 2005.
Children's Act 38 of 2005.
Civil Union Act 17 of 2006.
Consumer Protection Act 68 of 2008.
Companies Act 71 of 2008.

Law Commission Working Papers and Reports

South African Law Commission: Working Paper on Domicile (Project 60) 1987.
South African Law Commission: Report on Domicile (Project 60) 1990.
South African Law Commission: Report on Domestic Arbitration (Project 94) 1998.
South African Law Commission: Report on Customary Law (Project 90) 2003.
South African Law Reform Commission: Issue Paper on Consolidated Legislation pertaining to Co-operation in Civil Matters (Project 121) 2003.
South African Law Reform Commission: Discussion Document on Consolidated Legislation pertaining to Co-operation in Civil Matters (Project 121) 2004.

Conventions

New York Convention on the Recognition and Enforcement of Foreign Arbitral Awards (1958).
Draft Hague Convention on the Formal Validity of Wills (1960).
Hague Convention on the Recognition of Divorces and Legal Separations (1968).
The Convention on the Law Applicable to Contractual Obligations (1980) (Rome Convention).
Hague Convention on the Civil Aspects of International Child Abduction (1980).
Hague Convention on Protection of Children and Co-operation in respect of Intercountry Adoption (1993).

Selected Bibliography

Regulations

EC Regulation 593/2008 on the Law Applicable to Contractual Obligations (Rome I)
EC Regulation 864/2007 on the Law Applicable to Non-contractual Obligations (Rome II)

Index

The numbers here refers to paragraph numbers.

www.ingramcontent.com/pod-product-compliance
Lightning Source LLC
Chambersburg PA
CBHW071350230926
51846CB00002B/502
* 9 7 8 9 0 4 1 1 5 1 8 0 3 *